IMPACT WITH INTEGRITY

IMPACT
WITH
INTEGRITY

*Repair the World
Without Breaking Yourself*

BECKY MARGIOTTA

Foreword by Dr. Kathlyn Hendricks
Preface by Susan X Jane

GIRL FRIDAY BOOKS

GIRL FRIDAY BOOKS

Published by Girl Friday Books™, Seattle
www.girlfridaybooks.com

Produced by Girl Friday Productions

Design: Rachel Marek
Project management: Sara Spees Addicott
Editorial production: Jaye Whitney Debber

Cover image © komkrit Preechachanwate/Shutterstock

Excerpt on pages 111–12 reproduced by permission from Caroline Hill,
The Big 10 (+1) Ideas that Fuel Oppression (https://medium.com/equity
-design/the-big-10-1-ideas-that-fuel-oppression-97d7200929f9, 2017).

Table on pages 116–18 reproduced by permission from
Kathy Obear, Privileged and Marginalized Identities
(Social Justice Training Institute, 2010).

Appendix A reproduced by permission from Kathlyn
Hendricks, F.A.C.T. Process (Hendricks Institute, 2017).

Appendix B reproduced by permission from Kathlyn
Hendricks, Persona Interview (Hendricks Institute, 2003).

ISBN (hardcover): 978-1-954854-27-7
ISBN (e-book): 978-1-954854-28-4

Library of Congress Control Number: 2021920209

First edition

For Christine and the two amazing human beings she brought into this world, our children, Huck and Vivian.

CONTENTS

FOREWORD

By Dr. Kathlyn Hendricks

Humans get notice periodically that "This is it!" This is the most critical, pivotal moment in human history. Maybe in retrospect historians will find another era where so much was at stake, but right now you couldn't find a better guide than this book to landing in your leadership and contributing to our world. This. Is. It.

Personal change is not enough anymore. Tending your own garden isn't enough. Systemic change that accounts for variables, resistance, and the unknown is needed to transform society.

Some people lead brilliantly but can't teach others how to do what flows from them so effortlessly. Many people talk a good game but sputter out at the street level of implementation. Others inspire transformation in short bursts but can't maintain change. Becky Margiotta both inspires and sustains and can show you how to scale true contextual change.

Becky can show you how to tend your own garden so you can create even more impactful systemic change. So many of us want to change the world, and so many of us have hurled our well-being and life balance onto the sacrificial pyre, believing that doing good must use us up. In *Impact with Integrity*, you'll learn how to be well while being of service. I know, I know.

It sounds like another do-gooder manifesto with no legs. But what most people who want to make a difference don't realize is that you need to *be* the difference first, and then allow the difference to move through you. In this book, you can enter a new world of contribution while filling your personal reservoir.

Becky's résumé is an adventure novel in itself, but you'd never know it from her unpretentious demeanor unless her experience bears directly on the issue at hand. In which case, she can laser beam the relevant experience or parachute in the exact statistics and places where it worked. She does a kind of shape-shifting that we usually only experience in action-hero movies. Like a magnet arranging iron filings around itself, Becky's focus and commitment align her choices to generate real power, the power of full engagement. She'll show you how to unleash your genius and make it funny. She'll get in your face with relentless authenticity and then walk with you through the door that's always been there behind all the secrets and self-criticism most people employ to motivate themselves. She's done the work, put in the hours, and honed the craft, and you can get it all by osmosing what speaks to you most.

This isn't so much a book to stuff into your mind as a rollicking whole-body, whole-mind, and wholehearted adventure to enjoy. You'll find hidden doors, chutes-and-ladders moves, mirrors, and puzzles to transform your way of acting effectively in the world. Becky addresses the most important collective issues at this pivotal point in human history, emphasizing the value of full-spectrum feeling and the justice imperative that each of us can meet and cocreate through responsibility. There's a lot of evidence that systemic suppression of feeling lurks in the basement of most conflict and power struggles. Becky invites you to genuinely befriend all the musty corners of your personal feelings closet and embrace presence and powerful engagement. She guides you through the overview and the right-now elements of actually getting from here to your goal with a range of examples that always favor possibility through the portal of full authenticity. She's embodied openness to learning and stands toe-to-toe with you until you turn inward, welcome feedback, and collaborate toward genuine equality.

Here's the best part. There are nutrients on each page, bite-sized blessings you can easily receive and practice and use to access your genius to build structures that make your dreams real. You can go through the book chapter by chapter or just open to any page and apply the wisdom right now.

PREFACE

By Susan X Jane

The world is on fire and in desperate need of volunteer firefighters. If you have ever wondered if there was a purpose for you, a place in the world in need of your unique genius, the answer is yes. If you have ever wondered when the right time is to step into your purpose and explore the path of your potential, the answer is now. The "how" is in your hands—and within your power. You don't have to do that work alone. Becky has created in this book a doorway for you to look at yourself and the very local power you have and to hone that power to create large-scale social change.

In my work providing training and coaching for organizations looking to address culture, I always tell people to do their own work first. Do the internal work of checking your own beliefs and values and exploring how they contribute to the very world you seek to change. Frankly, I am often met with a blank stare: What does it mean to do your own work? Now I can just hand them *Impact with Integrity: Repair the World Without Breaking Yourself.* This book invites you to explore new ways of being, freeing you to create fluid and moving dynamics that can carry us to new places. Examining yourself is key to supercharging your power to make the world a better place.

Doing Your Own Work First

People eager to create change in the world are often powerfully motivated to find solutions to big, hairy problems, seeking an impactful action they can take to stop harm against the vulnerable. It seems odd, then, to look for solutions to these problems inside ourselves—we, after all, are the ones who want to help. Too often we start looking for answers by focusing our energy on fixing others, or on the problem right in front of us. If only we could change everyone else then all would be right with the world! Only it doesn't work that way. To make change, we must be the change. All change we wish to manifest, we must make first in ourselves. And that's the best part: all the power we need to make change begins right here, right inside each of us.

Leaders need to think about how they show up as leaders, because this shapes the environment in which the work will take place. Real change requires community, listening to and engaging with those we serve, and attention to the impact of our work. Without a real, authentic dialogic environment, the kind of communication needed to make lasting change in the world is unlikely to happen. Instead we take on the colonized norms—flawed mirrors of patriarchal white dominant culture. Leaders who create emotional spaces for themselves and others are able to build true community inside organizations, and give their teams the blueprints, skills, practice, and tools they need to create impact.

Calling Out Patriarchal White Supremacy

An important connection Becky helps us make through this book is that often internal dynamics are deeply informed by the culture we live in, namely patriarchal white supremacy.

Our interactions, particularly around power and in spaces where inequity exists, are defined by the dominant values of the culture we are in—we are fish *in* water, sometimes privileged to swim our whole life without recognizing the ways that patriarchal white supremacist norms have defined our modes of interacting, communicating, and building together. Old ways of getting and maintaining power are centered in concepts of scarcity thinking, "us versus them" mentality, and control from the top down.

We reinforce existing power structures with every interaction. Leaders who make environments for others decide the kind of power relationships that will exist among those being helped and those helping. Even when we seek to help, we can reinforce ways of being that disregard the communities we seek to serve and center us instead in our personal power. Every time we exercise power, we decide whether we live authentically in a place that recognizes the humanity in others or not.

Liberating ourselves from old ways of thinking frees us to develop new ways of being. There is no shame here in calling out the norms we operate within, but there is great power in breaking those norms in favor of real transformation. Making connections between the macro- and microcosm can create integrity and alignment with our mission personally and professionally. Indeed, leaders who examine themselves and the hegemonic ideology shaping their environment can maintain a vision for their organizations that will subvert dominant norms, work to dismantle harmful structures rather than replicate existing power dynamics, and create a fertile environment for change.

The work you do here with Becky will help you draw connections between dysfunctional personal and workplace dynamics and patriarchal white supremacist values. Beginning to unpack the existing ways of thinking and moving yourself into new spaces will enable you to instead create change free from fear and silence with a foundation of solidarity, connection, love, and abundance.

INTRODUCTION

My college professor Colonel Jay Parker started every course he taught, every single semester, by recounting the story of Gertrude Stein on her deathbed. As the story goes, Gertrude's friends were wanting to bring her comfort however they could. At one point, she mustered the strength to ask, "What is the answer?" Bewildered, her friends were unable to satisfy her with their responses. So Gertrude said, "Well, then, what is the question?" Then she died.

As social change leaders, we need to ask useful questions. Asking good questions can be even more important than having good answers. And it is with that spirit of humble inquiry in mind that I offer a *big* question to you. It's the one I bring into my own work with social change leaders from all over the world:

> **How do you take healthy responsibility not just for yourself but for the whole of the web of life?**

I don't have a specific answer to this question. It is a touchstone for me; it's something I come back to again and again.

(And you'll see me revisit it throughout this book.) I believe answering this question is the defining challenge of our time. I believe the survival of humanity depends upon our ability to rise to the occasion, both as social change leaders and as humans.

Knowing that we are inextricably intertwined, knowing that we are swimming in a pool of oppression that we didn't create, knowing that there is tremendous suffering in the world and that the only thing that might make a difference is to step into healthy responsibility for the whole, what else is there to do but wrap our arms around the world's biggest problems and bite off as much as we can chew?

One of the earliest definitions of leadership I used was this: it's getting people to do something they don't want to do. I am guilty myself sometimes—and I know I'm not alone—of asking in frustration, "How can I get all these people to do what *I* want them to do?"

Unfortunately, this way of thinking about leadership and making change in the world is all too common. Implicit in that framework is a mental model of manipulation, power, and coercion. That is not leadership, at least not in my book.

The best definition of leadership that I've encountered I learned from LaShawn Chatmon at the National Equity Project. They define leadership as taking responsibility for what matters to you.

Full stop. Period.

The leadership paradigm I will lay out in this book builds upon this notion of taking responsibility for what matters to you. I offer it in direct contrast to the more traditional "power-over" forms of so-called leadership.

For many years, I was inspired by this Buckminster Fuller quote: "If we are any good at problem-solving, we don't come to utopia, we come to more difficult problems to solve." Now don't get me wrong. I still love this notion, but part of what

I want to offer here is a shift in orientation from "What's wrong?" to "How can we create even more connections across the web of life?"

With each step we take into healthy responsibility for ourselves, we grow not only in our capacity to notice and experience the profound spiritual truth that we are connected but also in our ability to notice exactly *how* everything is connected. We align our presence with our purpose. Over time, we vector our way into "right relationship" with one another and the earth. This is my best hypothesis about how we might go about weaving together the web of life.

What if all we need to do as leaders is this: take healthy responsibility for what matters to us, as we grow increasingly attuned to the complexity of the web of life and expand in our ability to weave authentic connections.

Lather, rinse, repeat.

I'm talking about committing to a lifelong journey toward wholeness that extends far beyond the confines of our physical bodies, because there's really no such thing as "me" that's separate from the whole in the first place. This book is an invitation for you to explore exactly how you might go about doing this, if it speaks to you.

I want you to be able to successfully navigate the Mad Hatter tea party that we refer to as "business as usual." I invite you to try on for size an entirely new paradigm for defining what you are called to do as a social change leader, and that is to step into healthy responsibility for yourself first, for all your choices and actions. Doing so will better position you to then extend that outward, rippling in every direction through the interconnected, interwoven, inextricably linked web of life.

This book is lovingly written for people who are committed to making the world a better place. Activists, nonprofit leaders, community volunteers, educators, health care providers, government administrators, foundation managers—I'm talking to you. I am also writing this for people who might not yet call themselves activists or might not be working in the sectors listed above but who are change agents nonetheless. I'm writing this for anyone willing to bring their authentic self into whatever arena they find themselves in right now. I want them to be happy, love their work, and kick ass big-time, what-ever it is they do. I want them to be more effective and feel freer as a result of putting what I am going to share with them here to good use.

What to Expect in This Book

This approach to leadership starts by doing the inner work first. In fact, the first three of the four steps in our approach—Facing Your Challenges, Embracing Your Power, and Clarifying Your Commitment—fall exclusively within the domain of inner work. Only in the fourth step, Shifting Your Context, will you move into action that involves others.

And though what I will share might turn some of your thinking about your own leadership practice inside out, and invite you to question . . . well, everything, I am living proof that this path is filled with a whole bunch of laughter and joy, too.

This book will ask you to face into (and by this I mean con-front directly) what might be very uncomfortable truths about the world, your organization, and yourself, and then invite you to do something about it.

A lot of what I suggest goes against the grain of our culture:

- That work has to be hard
- That if we're not suffering, we won't be effective
- That it's unprofessional to be emotional at work
- That it's more important to be polite than to be real

This book is going to challenge these assumptions because they're sucking the life out of all of us. I will ask you to reconsider the way you think things should be and reevaluate how you want to show up in the world.

Most of the solutions I propose require you to take on some risk. That risk will vary depending on the extent to which our society privileges or has marginalized aspects of your complex identity. Some of you, like me, have more unearned privilege and can take bigger risks with fewer consequences. Some of you, based solely on your identity, will face more severe consequences for the same risks. Just because that's not fair doesn't make it not so.

This book will walk you through the framework for doing the inner work of social change that I share with leaders through the Billions Institute. Like a well-built house, I feel confident that the framework is a firm foundation to support you in doing whatever it is that you are here on this planet to do. You will soon discover this book is short on answers and long on questions. It is not my place to answer these questions for you, but to give you the framework for self-inquiry and suggest some ways of thinking about these questions that I have found helpful on my own journey. Just because this framework has been useful for me doesn't mean it will be useful for you. I encourage you to try it on for size, then keep what works for you and discard anything that doesn't.

The framework is meant to be done sequentially and is presented as such.

That said, I also believe in magic, so it's entirely possible that you could randomly open to any page and find exactly what you are looking for. Ultimately, this is a choose-your-own-adventure kind of book, but with a clear road map in case you want to forgo any narrative detours.

In each chapter, you will find several Act Now sections. These are reflection prompts and worksheets meant to be done

concurrently with that chapter, as a way to deepen and person-
alize your learning. If you would like to receive a consolidated
PDF of all the Act Now sections, go to www.billionsinstitute
.com/impactwithintegrity and I encourage you to download
one immediately. If you want to deepen your learning on this
subject, my company, the Billions Institute, offers courses for
social change leaders who are integrating these powerful concepts into their work to repair the world.

PART I:
FACE YOUR CHALLENGES

To "face" means to look at something directly, to be willing to fully grasp and absorb what is happening right here, right now. Not just with your mind or your eyes but with your whole being. Essentially, facing is being fully present and giving your attention to what is.

It seems simple and obvious, but most of the time we're not fully present to the way things are. There are many ways we don't fully face what's actually happening. We see things the way we want to see them, instead of how they are.

We spin stories.

We flee backward to a (better) past.

We flee forward into a (better) future.

We look away or hide our eyes from the full picture.

We get distracted by squirrels.

But nothing can be changed until you face it.

In this part, I'm going to walk you through how you can start doing the inner work of social change by facing your challenges. First, we will dive into the "why" of working on yourself first and what it means to really take part in doing that inner work. Then, we'll unpack the four most common organizational challenges that I've observed in the hundreds of organizations I've worked with in my seminars:

- Indecision
- Blame and criticism
- Micromanagement
- Overwork and overwhelm

Finally, we will inquire whether these organizational toxins have deeper roots in broader societal forces of oppression.

Sometimes your challenge is with one person, and you can resolve it in one sweaty-palmed conversation.

Sometimes your challenge involves many people participating in a toxic organizational dynamic.

Sometimes your challenge is a deeper, more systemic, and structural one that bumps up against oppressive societal norms.

Regardless of which challenges you choose to face, each is an invitation to step more fully into becoming a leader who takes full responsibility for every situation you find yourself in. Period.

Facing reality head-on can be hard. Some people spend their whole lives in denial or willful ignorance. But until you do, you cannot repair the world. When you face a situation fully, you must be willing to see your role in keeping it going, however minor. It's only once you look at it that you can open up the possibility of creating something new and different in the world. And that's what leading change is all about.

For some of us, this first step of facing can be overwhelming and heighten our anxiety. My meditation teacher, Sylvia Boorstein, often says, "May I meet this moment fully, may I meet it as a friend." I want to invoke Sylvia's friendly clause here and encourage you to face whatever you have been avoiding, and to do so in a way that honors your own process and is appropriately kind and gentle to yourself.

CHAPTER 1

WHY DO THE INNER WORK?

So there I was, an army first lieutenant stationed in Hawaii. During peacetime, we'd "go to the field" every few weeks and practice what we'd do if we were called to war. We'd simulate things as realistically as possible. Everyone took it all very seriously. My job at the time was in the Systems Control Center that managed the communications network for the Twenty-Fifth Infantry Division. I was all of twenty-five years old, and I was the lowest-ranking officer in the Systems Control Center. So I drew the short stick of working the night shift.

We tracked the entire network with green and red magnets on a dry erase board. Green meant the link between two sites was good. Red meant the link was down and the commanders at those sites couldn't communicate with the rest of the division. My job—my only job—was to keep those links green. One night around 2:00 a.m. we received our first notice that one of the major links had gone down. Then another. Then another. Then another. My stomach sank. One after another, the entire network turned red as I watched helplessly.

We did everything we could to fix things, but what was happening was a catastrophic network failure. By 3:00 a.m. every single link in the network was red. We were totally screwed.

At this point, my colleagues and I realized that we needed to wake the colonel and let her know what was happening. She would be in the hot seat come morning because each day promptly at 7:00 a.m. she attended an in-person briefing with the division commander. As our leader, she would definitely be held to account for what was happening. She deserved to know, but nobody wants to wake up the boss at three in the morning. You save that for when it's bad. But this was one of those times.

As we debated what to do, we did what all civilized people do when they reach an impasse. We played rock, paper, scissors. Rock beat scissors. It fell on me to wake up the colonel.

So I slinked into her quarters, knocked gently on the door, and said, "Ma'am, I'm so sorry to wake you up, but we need you in the headquarters; the network is *down*." She got up and quickly joined us in the Systems Control Center, where we stood completely defeated in front of that dry erase board with all those red magnets. We briefed her and she took it all in, then paused for a moment; I grabbed my pen and paper, ready to jot down her instructions.

The colonel nodded her head and seemed to understand the gravity of the situation. And I promise you I was *not* expecting what happened next. She poked me in the chest four times and said, *"Unfuck this, Lieutenant."*

No pressure, right? At that moment, I knew I had a big problem to solve. The question was how to solve it (and solve many more big problems later) without losing myself in the process.

Unfortunately, these kinds of super-stressful situations are far from rare. They happen all the time, so much so that we tend to accept them as simply a part of life. In an ideal world, these moments would be rare. And yet, for many of us, we get up in the morning, throw ourselves into the work, and at the end of a long day look in the mirror and realize tomorrow we have to do the same thing all over again. When these kinds of events become chronic, we enter the realm of burnout.

Doing the work of social change every day is admirable. But you also have to do the inner work every day, too. By "inner work," I mean that you need to fix what isn't working on the inside before you can begin to address what isn't working on the outside, in the greater web of life. Let's explore some reasons why you should do the inner work.

Reason #1: If You Don't Do the Inner Work, You'll Burn Out

I know a thing or two about burnout myself. Let me tell you how I got there. Maybe you can relate. In 2007, I was working on the problem of street homelessness for the absolutely brilliant and amazing Rosanne Haggerty. She is someone I will be grateful for knowing for the rest of my life. Rosanne had hired me to reduce street homelessness by two-thirds in three years in Times Square, and we were making great progress. So she offered me a promotion. "You're good at start-ups," she said. "Will you oversee all our new initiatives?" To which, without hesitation, I answered with an enthusiastic yes. My new job title was director of innovations.

Before I knew it, I had nine direct reports, all of whom were managing what could be considered the "high risk" or "double secret probation" portfolio of the organization.

One project I was responsible for was laying the groundwork for a housing program for homeless veterans in recovery in upstate New York. So every couple of weeks I'd travel up there (getting carsick each time) only to have community members scream at me about how I personally was going to bring murderers and rapists to their neighborhood by advancing this housing program.

Meanwhile, the small, privately funded pilot program on street homelessness I had originally been hired to direct was so successful that New York City recalled $10 million in contracts from all their providers and essentially said, "If you want our money, you have to do what Becky's small pilot program is doing." So I spent the next few months helping organizations that I wanted to see succeed in other boroughs write proposals to completely overhaul NYC's street outreach program. All the proposals I helped write were selected, and overnight, the team that had started with just me and an AmeriCorps volunteer grew to over thirty people. The approach we had created had spread to all five boroughs of the largest city in the United States.

Over the next few months, I continued to support the ramp-up of that newly expanded program and the eight other programs I was overseeing. Plus I was banging out grad school on nights and weekends. Over time, I found myself working past midnight on a regular basis, skipping the gym, gaining weight, feeling exhausted, and growing resentful. It was all too much. Burnout was inevitable. I knew I was making an impact—but at what cost?

When all of this was happening back in 2006 and 2007, I assumed it was (a) happening to me, and (b) happening to me alone. Little did I know a lot of my fellow workers in the nonprofit sector were experiencing burnout, too. This burnout has been the subject of much study over the past few years. For example, in 2020, The Wellbeing Project produced an in-depth report called "How Changemakers' Inner Wellbeing Influences Their Work." It's worth reading the entire thing cover to cover, but I want to share a few highlights with you.

One study of nonprofits' and NGOs' employees found that 42 percent of respondents believed their job was detrimental to their mental health. Another study found that individuals in the "helping" professions (nurses, doctors, teachers, and therapists) are prone to a high level of trauma and depression due to the nature of their work because it requires them to care for others. In a 2015 study of human rights advocates, 19 percent met the criteria for PTSD diagnosis, while 15 percent met the threshold for depression.

Lest we think this is only relevant for those working in the medical or mental health fields, it's not. A 2020 survey of over 1,300 active-duty law enforcement officers from across the US found that 59 percent of those surveyed reported feeling trapped or hopeless about their jobs. Forty-seven percent tested positive for PTSD—about nine to ten times greater than the general population.

I was experiencing many of the effects of this culture of overwork and overwhelm every single day. And believe me, I attempted some misguided strategies to remedy the situation. Luckily, I didn't resort to drugs or alcohol, but I've never met a slice of pizza that didn't have my name on it. I worked later and later into the evening to get through my inbox. I used my vacation time to finally get caught up on work. I even took a two-day time management course and got a fancy notebook planner thingy, which I used diligently for all of two weeks.

If you're like me, you went into this work to have an impact. What happens instead, though, is that too many of us end up bolting for the door. Another study of 10,000 nonprofit professionals found that more than 90 percent of respondents regarded burnout as the principal reason for leaving the sector. In other words, we are taking on an abundance of responsibility in an unhealthy way. We bear it mentally, physically, spiritually, and emotionally. We can't fix it all, nor can we bear it all. That's a lesson I learned the hard way.

The headline here (and the entire point of this book) is that all the overwhelming things I described above weren't happening *to* me. Quite the opposite. I was an active participant, albeit unconsciously, in creating the conditions for burnout in my life. By doing the inner work that I will teach you how to do in this book, I was able to take healthy responsibility for my choices and actions and dig myself out of the rut I was in. I'll tell you all about how I did that in chapter 11, but there's one more big problem when we fail to do the inner work that we have to talk about first.

Reason #2: If You Don't Do the Inner Work, You'll Have Less Impact

In the summer of 2013, I found myself in Nashville, Tennessee, being interviewed by none other than Anderson Cooper. It was surreal. Bright lights shining in my face, cameras rolling. Out of the corner of my eye I could see my communications director, Jake Maguire, giving me the thumbs-up.

60 Minutes was doing a story on the 100,000 Homes Campaign that I directed for Community Solutions from 2009 to 2014. This campaign mobilized 186 cities in the United States to house 105,000 people who had been living on the streets in just under four years.

There's a saying that when *60 Minutes* calls, don't answer. The reason people say that is because *60 Minutes* is one of the few remaining investigative journalism operations in the United States, and they are notoriously thorough. It is not uncommon for a *60 Minutes* piece to come back and bite you in the ass. We knew we were solid, though, and when it aired in the spring of 2014, not only did they give our campaign glowing remarks, but they also filmed an additional segment about how doing this story changed Anderson Cooper's own perceptions about the issue of homelessness.[1]

Huge victory for the cause, right? Unquestionably, yes.

And yet, there are things I said or perhaps, more important, things I neglected to say in that interview that haunt me to this day. For example, I failed to mention the role that structural racism plays in perpetuating homelessness in the United States. At the time, I had not fully faced into this reality in my own analysis, which rendered my work less effective than it might have been otherwise.

I am also haunted by how much I messed up the answer to one question in particular. Anderson Cooper must have asked me a dozen times different variations of the same question: "Do these homeless people deserve housing?"

Anderson Cooper wasn't the only person who had questions for me. When people found out I worked on street homelessness, the most common question they had was "Should I give them money?" The second most common question people asked was "Don't some people just *want* to be homeless?" And now here's Anderson Cooper asking me FAQ #3: "Do these people even deserve housing?"

Working on the issue of street homelessness for eleven years gave me some proximity to a tremendous amount of human suffering. I have been up close and personal and in

---

1. There is a debate among those in my former field about whether the most respectful and appropriate term to describe the situation of not having a permanent place to live is "houseless" or "homeless." I have never been comfortable with using the word "homeless" as an adjective, as in a "homeless person." There is much more to any human being than their housing status. And I very much appreciate the desire to acknowledge the many different forms of home that do not require a permanent structure. Language matters. I have consciously chosen to use the term "homeless" and "homelessness" in this book because it was how we spoke about it at the time, and changing my language retroactively would feel inauthentic to me. The important conversation happening around language used in this space remains ongoing and evolving.

relationships over time with people whose physical, mental, emotional, and, dare I say, spiritual anguish was at times overwhelming for me. I rode the train to and from work each day, and most days I'd hold it together until I got off the subway and was walking home by myself in the dark. That's when it would hit me. I would often find myself sobbing over what I had witnessed during the day. I was emotionally consumed by my work. I knew names and faces and stories of dozens of people that I could draw upon to answer Anderson's question.

Not only did I have dozens of stories to inform my answer, but I was also *that person* with my nose in a peer-reviewed journal during my daily commute. I read everything I could find about substance abuse, mental health, trauma, poverty, child welfare, cognitive impairment, housing, HIV/AIDS, domestic violence, school failure, veterans, and incarceration. You name it, I had read the latest peer-reviewed journal article on it. I even kept a diagram of all the cooccurring causes and chutes and ladders of factors related to homelessness. I wanted—I *needed*—to understand why homelessness existed and what could be done to end it.

Anderson Cooper had found the right person for his question. Or so you'd think.

Here's what I said in that moment: "It's not so much about whether or not they deserve housing, so much as what's best for all of us." Then I pivoted to an answer I had given hundreds of times before about how housing people actually generates a significant cost savings when compared to not doing so. This is true, by the way, mostly because hospital bills are way higher than the cost of renting a crappy apartment.

Anderson asked that same question again. And again. And again. It was beginning to remind me of my "how to survive foreign government detention" training when I was in the army.

Another time I responded, "I think most people, when given a second chance, deserve it and do well with it."

This final answer seemed to fit their narrative, and that is what you'll see if you watch the clip (which can be found here: https://www.youtube.com/watch?v=LEu2w1FtWME).

Had I done the inner work I'm going to teach you how to do, my answer would have been completely different and potentially far more impactful. But I hadn't done it yet. I was swimming in a sea of emotion, guilt, and savior narratives. I was not yet taking healthy responsibility for myself or how I interacted with my work.

What I wish I had said that day would go something like this:

> Anderson, I get that question often, and here's the problem with it: It assumes homeless people are to blame for being homeless in the first place. It puts the blame entirely on them for their situation with no corresponding critique of you and me and everyone else and the ways we, too, are responsible for the existence of homelessness in our society. When you frame the question that way, it puts the burden on the individual who is experiencing the problem, rather than on the system that is creating the problem. A better question might be "Why is it that people experiencing homelessness don't receive the same housing subsidies as people who have homes (in the form of the mortgage income tax deduction)?"

I know it seems like a small thing, one answer to one question in one interview. But I assure you it is much more than that. At the time, I did not understand how the question itself was part of the problem. So I accepted its premise that people are to be blamed for their lack of housing and that it's OK to talk about that without any concurrent systemic analysis. These ideas are the underpinnings of white saviorism, and white saviorism is a big part of the problem. I kept white saviorism going instead of pivoting to a deeper and more accurate analysis of homelessness. I'm not saying that to blame myself but to illustrate that something that can look like a success on the outside can actually be a failure or, at the very least, a significant missed opportunity. Had I done the inner work of social change, alarm bells would have gone off as soon as I heard Anderson's question and I would have answered it differently.

The core of this inner work is the act of taking healthy responsibility for all our choices and actions. When we take healthy responsibility, we ask better questions, and we demand better answers. We are better equipped to understand root causes and more likely to design useful solutions. I believe taking healthy responsibility—on an individual and collective level—is at the heart of what it means to be an effective social change agent. Let me break it down for you a little further.

Taking Healthy Responsibility

I learned about the concept of healthy responsibility from my mentor Dr. Kathlyn Hendricks during a two-year apprenticeship program that I did with her from 2012 to 2013. Kathlyn, along with her husband, Gay, has published more than forty books, trained thousands of coaches, appeared on *Oprah*, and hosted seminars across the globe. Almost a decade after I completed my apprenticeship with her, we are still friends and still talking about all the ways responsibility is the central challenge of our time. Kathlyn even likes to spell it "response-ability" to highlight that it is an ability or a skill one can learn versus an obligation or admonition that we bark at children so they will "be more responsible." It's so much more than that.

In its most simple form, responsibility is an ongoing choice to respond to each moment as it arises. Being responsible is not a one-and-done kind of thing; it is a way of being in the world. It is deceptively simple, and yet I don't think it's hyperbole to suggest the survival of humanity depends upon it.

Many people mistakenly refer to healthy relationships as being a fifty-fifty split of responsibility. If each person gives their 50 percent, so the story goes, all will be well. Problems only arise when one partner gives less than 50 percent. Kathlyn has a different take (one I agree with) that in healthy relationships, whether they be personal or professional, both partners take 100 percent (or healthy) responsibility for the relationship. Implicit in this notion is the understanding that each of us is a whole, complete person who is capable of taking ownership for every choice we make and every action we take in our lives. The invitation is to take responsibility for everything in our lives. Period.

Following this logic, when we're *not* in healthy responsibility, we're ceding that territory to someone or something else, living or dead, real or imagined. There are three basic orientations toward that "someone or something other than us" element that we hand responsibility over to:

1. You can be "at the effect of" something outside yourself. What this means is you locate responsibility for your choices and actions with someone or something other than yourself. For example, earlier in this chapter I wrote that I believed the conditions of burnout were happening to me. And when you're out of healthy responsibility, it feels just like that—as if life is happening *to* you. Even

though I know I have agency and control over my choices and actions, I forget that from time to time. And I imagine sometimes you do, too.

2. Another way you may avoid healthy responsibility is when you get really good at identifying whose fault it is that things are the way they are. You can blame, shame, and criticize and then crank up the evening news while you're at it, because the news is really good at doing this, too. That's not to say that there aren't valid critiques of who or what forces are initiating or perpetuating harm to others—that is incredibly important. But there's a big difference between blaming homeless individuals for their situation and getting curious about the conditions that enable hundreds and thousands of people to be without somewhere to live in the first place. We know that blame and criticism don't change a darn thing. And yet, from time to time, I still look for whom to blame. I imagine you do, too.

3. The final way you may avoid healthy responsibility is running around trying to make things OK when you notice that you or others are suffering. You put Band-Aids on sucking chest wounds and reassure yourself that things are going to get better. It's hard to see anyone suffering. But you may not believe you have the power to actually stop the suffering, so you busy yourself with temporary fixes. It's not to say that the impulse to reduce suffering isn't an important one—it's the very definition of compassion. It's what kept me going every single day, no matter how hard I cried once I got off the subway train. But if the fixes are only temporary, or depend upon people "needing" you, then, like

Sisyphus, you're merely pushing boulders uphill so they can roll back down again.

Being out of healthy responsibility (and on the road to the burnout I mentioned earlier) sets in motion what Dr. Stephen Karpman, an American psychologist whose area of focus is transactional analysis, dubbed the Drama Triangle. Karpman's idea was that every drama has a Victim, a Persecutor, and a Rescuer. I learned about Karpman's Drama Triangle from Kathlyn Hendricks, who uses the terms Victim, Villain, and Hero, which is what you will see used throughout this book. I'll unpack the concept in full in chapter 4 so you can dig deeper into its working parts.

For now, though, know that when you are on the Drama Triangle, individually or collectively, you are on a fast track to burnout. You completely misdiagnose the root causes of your problems, charging ahead with the wrong solutions. Being on the Drama Triangle uses a lot of energy and attention, hindering your ability to pinpoint and address the real root cause of why the world needs repairing in the first place: systemic oppression.

The Role of Systemic Oppression in Social Change Work

As you learn more about how to take healthy responsibility for yourself and others, you will begin to notice that, while you do make an impact, social change work never ends. It never goes away. There is always more work to do. Ask yourself what it would take for you to work yourself out of your job. What conditions would be necessary for your labor and contributions to no longer be required?

*"Thank you very much, Becky, but it turns out
we have no more people sleeping on our streets."*

*"Thank you very much, Jeremy, but it turns out
nobody gets sick these days."*

*"Thank you very much, Nicole, but nobody dies
from gun violence anymore."*

*"Thank you very much, Lindsay, but actually
Black and Brown boys are thriving in our schools."*

*"Thank you very much, Arief, but we have the
perfect amount of CO2 in the atmosphere right
now."*

Can you imagine what that would feel like? It'd be incredible, right?

But you know it's probably not going to happen, at least not in our lifetime.

And while there are many complex reasons for that, I believe there's one main reason: we all live and work within a broader context of oppression. By oppression I mean the pressing down effect of the unjust exercise of force.

I should mention that I don't offer this analysis to blame, shame, or criticize, but rather as critique, to simply state with no judgment what is, from my admittedly limited perspective. Take any social issue that any of us have dedicated our lives to, then start peeling that onion for the underlying root causes, and eventually you will get to oppression.

Unfortunately, there is no single wizard-behind-the-curtains, nameable, finger-pointable thing that is oppression. That would be too easy. Yet everything we do rests on millennia of extracting labor from people without paying fairly for it and extracting resources from the earth without paying the full price of the externalities.

This fundamental injustice, this abuse of power, is simply, unfortunately, business as usual on planet Earth. If oppression didn't exist, the vast majority of us who find meaningful employment in the social sector would be out of a job. In fact, we have jobs precisely because of the broader context of oppression that created the conditions many of us accept as "normal."

Nobody signed up to work in the social sector to rearrange the deck chairs on the *Titanic*. And yet, that's what many of us do for a living. Whether, like me, you initially got involved in this work to escape your own suffering or for other reasons that are solely yours, once you realize that a lot of people don't have good choices to make, it becomes increasingly clear that your work is not just to put on Band-Aids but to stop the bleeding in the first place. Taking healthy responsibility for yourself first can give you the tools you need to address the systemic and oppressive root system that perpetuates the problems you're trying to solve.

What This Work Requires

So, dear reader, I'm glad you're here.

Though so many people are doing so many amazing things, the party is incomplete without you. To create the world we want requires your unique and full contribution, too. And we have so much work to do.

I have stood beside powerful change leaders as they have sobbed tears of despair over the suffering they have witnessed and their inability to stop it. This work requires emotional depth and resilience.

Years ago I missed the opportunity to tell the deeper and fuller truth about homelessness when I was interviewed by

Anderson Cooper for *60 Minutes*. This work requires more than good intentions.

I have lost track of how many powerful change leaders I've known who have quit their jobs because the conditions were too toxic. This work may cause you harm.

I know way too many powerful change leaders who are reluctant to fully interrogate systems and histories of oppression as well as how their own identities, biases, and power unwittingly perpetuate them. And sometimes that could be said about me, too. This work requires humility and curiosity out the wazoo.

It is possible to transform the world—or at least contribute substantially to it in the way that you were uniquely put on this earth to do. But we won't make progress "out there" until we take full ownership of what's going on "in here." That is the inner work of social change.

The only way I know how to do this work is to step into healthy responsibility, not just for myself, but for the whole shebang. Stay with me and I'll explain what I mean by that.

For years, I did my own inner work and got really good at getting off the Drama Triangle and taking healthy responsibility for myself. By that, I mean reliably taking healthy responsibility for every single one of my choices and actions. Honestly, it was as if I had acquired superpowers. I developed new skills that resulted in me playing a different game from many people around me. I learned how to organize myself differently, and in so doing I created a different context for myself. As I changed, my entire life changed along with me.

I have found that I can do all of these things:

- Reliably notice what body sensations and feelings I am experiencing in the moment
- Access my millions-of-years-old evolutionary "body intelligence"—that is, bring awareness to the

sensations in my body, make sense of their meaning, and use this source of wisdom to augment my
rational intelligence when I'm making decisions

- Detect almost instantly when I am, or someone
  else is, afraid
- Shift out of fear and into presence at will
- Disengage myself from and, with permission,
  help others to defuse most forms of interpersonal
  drama, freeing up a tremendous amount of creative energy for things that are more useful
- Stay open to learning and being curious, even when
  someone is saying something that I disagree with
- Speak what is true for me, in a way that often
  invites others into deeper connection and relationship with me
- Know what I care about, what I'm really good at
  doing, and what fuels my aliveness so I can spend
  most of my time "in my genius" (doing what I love
  and what I'm really good at)
- Consciously decide where to place my attention,
  including what to no longer give attention to
- Shift contexts at will, creating openings that are
  filled with new possibilities through my choice of
  words and actions

I wish I knew back in the military what I know now—that
walking away from the Drama Triangle and taking healthy
responsibility exponentially increases a person's impact as a
leader.

That's exactly what the colonel did that night in the systems room. Taking one look at the unfolding chaos, she did
the one thing no one in the room expected: she went back to
bed. She literally went back to bed. I remember it like it was
yesterday. I remember what I did. I took a deep breath. I looked

my colleagues in the eye. We looked at all those red links on the board. And we got to work unfucking things. That's it. That's all there is to the story. We simply got on with the work of unfucking things. By the time the colonel woke up in the morning, the network was green again.

Well, that's not really all there is to the story. Perhaps the most important part of the story is what she *didn't* do. She did not roll up her sleeves and take over like the Hero persona, though she certainly could have. She didn't have even the slightest shred of blame or criticism in her tone like the Villain persona. And she definitely didn't curl up into a ball and wish it all away like the Victim persona.

This is what happens when you bypass the Drama Triangle and instead just get to work. By simply telling me to unfuck this, she gave me a template for how to get big things done— big impact with no drama—at the tender age of twenty-five. It's not that I didn't feel scared or anxious (I certainly did before I woke her up). But because of the context and the colonel's unique, healthy responsibility–infused style of leadership, we were able to get the job done.

So I had to ask myself, How is this kind of impact possible now, even when you don't have a colonel poking you in the chest telling you to unfuck things? And it dawned on me that I've spent most of the last twenty-seven years of my life figuring out how to do just that—to create big impact with no drama.

You probably don't have the leeway to go around poking your colleagues in the chest four times demanding they unfuck things (but secretly, don't you wish you could?). But you want to have big impact with no drama, so I offer you here my best alternative: doing the inner work of social change.

The secret is in how you show up every day with your colleagues within and outside your organizations. It doesn't matter if you get a Super Bowl commercial if on the way to filming it you treat your colleagues like dirt. The key is to avoid getting sucked into the oppressive and fear-based contexts, and instead intentionally create new contexts of love, liberation, creativity, and possibility with every single interaction.

I want every person who is working in one form or another to repair the world to have everything they need to square off against oppression. To dismantle it piece by piece. To reclaim their agency, hold on to their creativity, and ground themselves in their humanity no matter what slings and arrows come their way.

If this is you, you've come to the right place. I want you to make your big dent in the universe.

It takes tremendous courage to dismantle these oppressive dynamics and do our own inner work as well. Yet, that is exactly what is required to create lasting social change. It can cost you your livelihood, and possibly even your life. It can be demoralizing and exhausting.

And, it's everything.

This. Is. The. Work.

I'll say it again:

This. Is. The. Work.

No matter what your risk tolerance may be, you still have agency.

So let's proceed together with care.

Act Now: Am I Ready to Do the Inner Work?

Take a few minutes and ask yourself the following questions:

Am I at a point in my life where I can be introspective and reflect on what's actually happening in the world and in my work? _____

Am I willing to tell myself the truth? _____

Am I open to learning whatever it is I want and need to learn from my situation? _____

Am I at a place emotionally and mentally where I'm able to face some things that might upset me? _____

Who are my allies and mentors I can count on for support?

_____

_____

_____

_____

_____

To the extent that I may be impacted by not having good choices in my life right now, am I nonetheless willing to acknowledge these barriers and still exercise my agency and power?

_____

Only you can answer these questions. Before you proceed, give these questions one more read through and consider your willingness to change old patterns that have been holding you back. Be honest with yourself.

Act Now: Self-Assessment on the Inner Work of Social Change

Now that you've taken some time to reflect, let's assess. Place a check mark by all the items listed below that are true for you now, and circle any items that are important for you to learn and integrate going forward.

☐ I reliably notice what body sensations and feelings I am experiencing in the moment.

- [ ] I access my millions-of-years-old evolutionary body intelligence and use it to augment my rational intelligence when I'm making decisions.
- [ ] I can detect almost instantly when I am, or someone else is, afraid.
- [ ] I shift out of fear and into presence at will.
- [ ] I disengage myself from and, with permission, help others defuse most forms of interpersonal drama, freeing up a tremendous amount of creative energy for things that are more useful.
- [ ] I stay open to learning and being curious, even when someone is saying something that I disagree with.
- [ ] I speak what is true for me, in a way that often invites others into deeper connection and relationship with me.
- [ ] I know what I care about, what I'm really good at doing, and what fuels my aliveness, and I spend most of my time in my genius.
- [ ] Perhaps most important of all: I can shift contexts at will. Through my choice of words and actions, I can create openings that are filled with new possibilities.
- [ ] I catch myself when I am feeling entitled and shift my awareness to appreciation.
- [ ] I notice when I am withholding important information from somebody and share my truth in a way that is unarguable (that is, it cannot be argued with).
- [ ] I say yes to what I experience, a "full-body yes." In other words, I only say yes when I am fully on board with something.
- [ ] I say no when I experience anything other than a full-body yes.

☐ I keep my agreements without needing to be reminded.

☐ I proactively change agreements that are no longer working for me.

☐ I choose whether or not I want to take action on any given issue and redirect my attention accordingly.

Chapter 1 Takeaways

• Failure to take healthy responsibility results in burnout and reduces our effectiveness as social change leaders.

• Responsibility is the ongoing choice to respond.

• Healthy responsibility means being fully accountable for 100 percent of your choices and actions.

• We sometimes avoid healthy responsibility by going on the Drama Triangle and seeing ourselves as being at the effect of something outside ourselves (Victim persona), blaming, shaming, or criticizing someone or something else (Villain persona), or providing temporary but unsustainable relief (Hero persona).

• Without oppression, there would be little or no need for the social sector.

• The inner work of social change requires us to step into healthy responsibility for every choice we make and every action we take.

CHAPTER 2

THE INNER WORK OF SOCIAL CHANGE

I hope from the previous chapter I've made it exceedingly clear that you won't make progress "out there" until you take healthy responsibility for everything you're experiencing "in here." If you neglect or shortchange the inner work, your effectiveness as a social change leader will be minimal and it's likely that you will make things worse, despite your best intentions. But how can you take healthy responsibility? What exactly is the inner work? In this chapter, I'm going to explain exactly what the four steps of the inner work are that enable you to get off the Drama Triangle and shift into healthy responsibility.

So let's dig into what doing the inner work looks like. You will be using this framework in the chapters ahead (and we'll dive deeper into each step as we go). Here, I'm going to use a story about one of the most difficult leadership challenges I faced as the director of the 100,000 Homes Campaign to walk you through each step. As you read, I want to encourage you to think about some of the biggest leadership challenges you're facing and begin to make connections to your own work.

Step 1: Face Your Challenges

A year and a half into what was supposed to be a three-year initiative for the 100,000 Homes Campaign, we finally conducted a thorough analysis of our performance data. Analyzing housing placement rates across more than one hundred participating cities enabled us to make accurate predictions about whether or not we were on track with our goal of helping communities move 100,000 people off the streets and into housing by July 2013. We had been working really hard for months and months, so I expected a rosy report.

Imagine my complete panic when my colleague Paul Howard told me that we were on track not to be the 100,000 Homes Campaign, but to be the 30,000 Homes Campaign.

How was it that I, entrusted with the responsibility of leading a campaign to house 100,000 people left to die on the streets of the United States, didn't know every single moment of every single day how many people had been moved into housing by the participating cities?

Ignorance is bliss, that's how. Plus we were busy. *Really* busy. And we were passionate about our cause! But mostly, I avoided facing into the data because I was afraid of failure.

What if we were behind? (Which we were.)

What could we possibly do differently? We were already stretched so thin and working so hard.

We couldn't do anything differently. That is, until I faced this challenge head-on.

Looking back, this was *the* defining moment of our campaign. Despite all our passion and dedication at the beginning, when it was all said and done, we jokingly referred back to ourselves in the early months as "clowns on the bus." Hard work and good intentions are a start, but insufficient for implementing real change.

At this turning point, we embraced a new motto: Face into the data. Face early. And face often. From that point forward, until the conclusion of the campaign, we started every single weekly team meeting by literally facing into the data on the three metrics that mattered most. Then we would spend most of the remainder of our time discussing strategies and tactics based on what the data were telling us. This was not your typical snooze fest staff update meeting. Think of it more like social change improv grounded by cold, hard facts. And it made all the difference in our ultimate success. That was my challenge to face—but what is yours?

The inner work of leading social change starts with looking squarely at what the heck is going on. In my case, I was avoiding facing our imminent failure, but that is just one of many challenges you might fail to face as you are leading change. There is no limit, really, to all the things that could possibly go wrong. So let's face that first. Ask yourself:

- What's keeping you up at night?
- What's not working?
- What's the problem "out there"?

Then assume you work on a team that is part of an organization and therefore is vulnerable to one or more of the four most common toxic organizational dynamics in the social sector: indecision, blame and criticism, micromanagement, and overwork and overwhelm.

Are you leaking precious life energy (energy that could otherwise be single-mindedly devoted to repairing the world) by allowing any of those toxic contexts to persist on your team or in your organization? If yes, let's face that, too.

Finally, expand your reflections to include the broader societal challenges of oppression that are associated with white supremacy culture. Before you think I'm only talking about the KKK or extremist groups, please bear with me and stay open to the possibility that what might actually be undermining your work to repair the world goes deeper than you had previously realized. Then ask:

- Are you creating the change you want to make in the world?
- Are you living in a way that is aligned with your deepest values?
- Are you leading in a way that is true to your most authentic self?

Considering all these factors will help you pinpoint the specific challenges you face. I should mention that some change leaders do not have the luxury of avoiding the data. Your lived experience and proximity to the suffering is all the data you need. For you, facing your challenges might be a softer look inside to your own pain and suffering and the necessary work of healing. For others, facing asks you to make a genuine effort to get proximate to the suffering of others so that you are not doing things *to* people but rather alongside and in solidarity with them. Wherever you are on the proximity spectrum, please remember to be compassionate with yourself and others.

Step 2: Embrace Your Power

It is one thing to fully face your challenge. It is another entirely to claim or reclaim your agency and choose to do something about it.

As soon as Paul told me we were on track to be the 30,000 Homes Campaign instead of the 100,000 Homes Campaign, without any conscious effort on my part, my brain started calculating excuses:

- *We've been so busy in the field doing the work, tracking the actual numbers just wasn't as important.*
- *We know we should have done this sooner, but we didn't have the right capabilities on our team.*
- *I mean, 30,000 is still pretty good, right? Maybe we were too ambitious in setting our goals.*

None of these excuses would have done a darn thing to get one more person into housing, but they offered me temporary psychological relief from my fear of failure. From my perch (on the Drama Triangle) it seemed as though things were happening *to me*. To our team.

In this case, I was clearly in the Victim position on the Drama Triangle, at the effect of I don't know what exactly. Let's just call it "forces beyond my control."

I knew I had to shift out of my Victim persona and back into my essence. By "essence," I mean my most authentic, grounded, natural state. Your essence is the point from which all sustainable social change flows.

One of my favorite ways to make this shift is to interview my persona to find out what it really wants. I called the Victim persona who showed up at that point in my life Don Piano based on the old-school *Sesame Street* character that flops his Muppet head on the piano keys when he (inevitably) can't remember the lyrics to a song. (It's worth Googling if you don't understand the reference.) When I interviewed my inner Don Piano persona (I'll teach you how to interview your own personas in chapter 4), I discovered that what I really wanted in my essence—more than for the campaign to succeed—was to alleviate the suffering of as many people living on the streets as possible. This return to purpose helped me get humble and stay curious as we navigated our next steps as a team.

Despite the personal drama and baggage you bring to the table, you still have power. You still have agency. You still have choices you can make and actions you can take. When you step off the Drama Triangle and into your essence, you are claiming or reclaiming your agency. You are no longer at the effect of forces outside yourself. You become a force to be reckoned with.

The key is to notice when you're on that Drama Triangle and get yourself off it as soon as you can. Whether you're in the Hero, Villain, or Victim position, nothing creative, transformative, or sustainable will result from your decisions or actions.

Next, you will conduct a clear-eyed assessment of your societal and positional power. In this particular situation for me, I had more than enough societal and positional power to plow right ahead. There were no disproportionate risks to me for stepping in and taking bold action. In fact, in this situation, given the amount of societal and positional power I had, it was all too tempting to rush in and try to fix everything myself because, well, I was the boss. And a white boss lady. Double trouble! When we have a lot of societal and positional power, the challenge is to slow our roll and cede power to others, lest we steamroll over them. It will be important for you to consider positional and societal power, too, and I'll help you do that in chapter 5.

Once you get off the Drama Triangle and back in your essence, but before you charge ahead with your plans, check in with your societal power. This is the power, or lack thereof, that is the result of the structures, both seen and unseen, within which you operate. The risks of taking action in this maldistributed power matrix will vary depending on how you are situated. Once you consider the implications, you can decide whether or not you actually want to do anything about the challenge. That, too, is a choice. One you and only you can make. That's your power at work.

Whether you ultimately decide to take action or not, you still proceed to the next step, clarifying your commitment.

Step 3: Clarify Your Commitment

Back to the 100,000 Homes Campaign . . .

Once I got off the Drama Triangle (thank you, Don Piano) and back into my essence, I decided that the best way to avoid ending up the 30,000 Homes Campaign was to involve the entire team. Fortunately, our next team retreat in Colorado was just a few weeks away.

In crafting our agenda, I set aside the entire first morning for the team to reckon with the data I had been given and make their own meaning of it. I didn't want to decide what to do next alone. I wanted that decision to be made and owned by the whole team. To their credit, the team enthusiastically embraced this new challenge. We had a solid track record of being able to get to consensus, but this time it was a little bit harder than usual because the stakes felt so high.

We entertained the possibility of adjusting our aim.

Maybe we should have been the 30,000 Homes Campaign all along. Maybe that's all that was ever possible anyway. Or maybe we should dilute whom we would count toward the target of 100,000 vulnerable people moving off the streets into homes.[2] It was very tempting to water things down in an attempt to be successful.

---

2. The term "vulnerable" can be problematic because it puts the emphasis on the individual rather than on the system; however, at the time, we used the term to describe people on the streets who had health conditions associated with a high mortality risk.

I had asked Paul to present the team with potential paths we might take to correct our course, and he came up with six options. We discussed those options for the rest of the morning. Everyone on the team leaned in with their very best ideas, but we weren't easily finding consensus about what to do next. Folks were getting hungry, and I said, "If we can't arrive at consensus when we come back from lunch, let's take it to a team vote."

But nobody on the team wanted to vote. Everybody wanted to stay with it and find consensus.

Then my colleague Linda Kaufman couldn't hold herself back anymore. She made a passionate plea to all of us to hold true to our values and our purpose and to not lose sight of why we were there in the first place: to expedite moving the most vulnerable people sleeping outside off the streets and into housing.

Linda's spontaneous outburst took us all out of our tactical, rational, decision-making mode and brought us back into our hearts and souls. She reminded us of what we had committed to at the beginning of the campaign. And that's the magic of clarifying your commitment. Once you reconnect with your deepest values and authentic wants, everything else becomes much clearer. This becomes your stake in the ground. It's your compass, your true north. Everything else easily flows from this center.

What Linda did in that moment was inspire our entire team to recommit to our original purpose. It was an honor to witness my colleague and friend show up so authentically in that moment. My job as the team leader wasn't to figure everything out and pop out of a cake with the solution to our challenge. My job was to get clear on my own commitment and then create the space for my teammates to do the same on their own terms. I had to be a buffer against fear and the unknown long enough for all of us to arrive at (or return to) our shared purpose. Once it became clear that we had a shared commitment again, our power to effect change multiplied exponentially.

Once you embrace your power and choose whether or not you want to take action, you, too, can clarify your commitment. To clarify your commitment, you must get out of limbo—just like we did in that team meeting. Being in limbo means you have some nagging ambivalence, something unresolved that is keeping you from being able to land wholeheartedly in a commitment. When you are in limbo, you are subject to the strongest forces in the room, including, among many other things, the seduction of going for the outward appearance of success while diluting your impact.

With a clear commitment, you become a force to be reckoned with. But it doesn't just happen.

The route to a clear commitment goes through the station called "feeling your feelings." There is no escaping this. I am going to take you through several exercises later in the book that help you unleash the mental clarity that can only be found on the other side of feeling your feelings. In part 3, you will start with exploring the subversive notion of using your own emotional intelligence to gain clarity about what you want, and then you will build upon that to unleash the power of commitment.

Once you've felt your feelings, you can start to ask yourself questions like these:

- What do I really want?
- What am I willing to do about it?
- What am I willing to commit to?

One of our fellows, Daisy Sharrock with the High Tech High Graduate School of Education, describes her experience of being clear in her commitment like this: *"I feel at peace/calm and know exactly how I want to respond in a given situation. I don't always have this clarity, but when I do, I know it. It usually means I am perfectly comfortable with whatever reactions others may have. I know that what I'm saying is my truth at that moment. There is alignment in my brain and body."*

This is what you are called to create room for as a leader. It is from this collaborative, generative spaciousness that you and your teams are best able to move your work forward.

When you have created that spaciousness, there is no time urgency. Sometimes it is best to take a pause and give yourself some room to gather additional information, either from the outside world or from your internal experience, so you can commit from a deeper place of essence.

Clarifying your commitment requires you to differentiate between your yeses and your nos, resolve your ambivalence, get clear on what you want and what you are willing to do, and commit to a direction. Your ability to commit is the most creative tool in your change leader toolkit.

Step 4: Shift Your Context

Facing the very real possibility of failure with the 100,000 Homes Campaign, we had aligned ourselves with our deepest values and recommitted to our aim of supporting cities in housing 100,000 of the most vulnerable people. But then what?

Once the team recommitted to our original purpose, Paul crunched some numbers and put some specifics to the course of action we had chosen together. If we could enroll three new communities every month, and if every community already in the campaign could double the monthly rate at which they were housing people, and if we gave ourselves an additional year, then we could achieve our goal to have 100,000 people in housing.

It sounds simple in retrospect, but those were some pretty big ifs. To execute them would require a complete reordering of our work, not to mention a significant change to our agreements with all of our stakeholders, including every funder, every partner, and each of the one hundred cities already enrolled in the campaign. So, reaching out to all our stakeholders to change our agreements with them became the priority for the team for an entire week. In other words, we shifted our context.

We call this "proactively changing agreements that no longer work for you," and it is one of several options on the menu for shifting the context. For us, that meant asking funders if we could extend our agreements by a year. We asked partners if they were still in for one more year. We asked cities if they were willing to commit to doubling the rate at which they moved people into housing and to making their housing placement rate public.

Fortunately, the funders and partners all said yes. Every city except one said yes. Then we completely overhauled our internal team operations to help those cities double their housing placement rates. And they did!

With this new plan, the campaign succeeded. The one hundred thousandth person moved into an apartment in April 2014. And thank goodness, because I had already gotten a tattoo with "100,00_ HOMES" on my left forearm. My plan was to get the final "0" added after the one hundred thousandth person moved into housing. Let's just say I had some skin in the game.

That's my story of how I (and my team) shifted context. But it's an idea that is widely studied, especially in relation to systemic change. In Donella Meadows's seminal article "Leverage Points: Places to Intervene in a System," she lists in increasing order of effectiveness ways we might go about transforming systems. She says, "The most stunning thing living systems and some social systems can do is to change themselves utterly by creating whole new structures and behaviors."

That is exactly what I mean by this notion of shifting the context: pulling your commitment forward into the real world through aligned actions to create new structures and behaviors.

If you think of yourself as being inextricably connected in this system called the web of life, then it makes a whole lot of sense for you to sharpen your skills in service of collective resilience and evolution. This is where the work of repairing the world gets tangible results.

Shifting the context means introducing something new that effectively changes the game. The current game is rigged. And as more and more of us translate our commitments into action, the current game loses power and a new one emerges.

I realize that shifting the context can seem rather vague and conceptual. The simplest way I can explain context is to compare it to an environment that you are creating, consciously or not. It is how you organize yourself and, in so doing, shape what enters into your awareness and how you engage with it. So shifting the context is intentionally reorganizing yourself into a new posture, perspective, or way of being and literally changing the game you and the people around you are playing. It's realizing everyone else is playing checkers, and you start playing a game of chess; it's the same board, but an entirely more sophisticated game. It is shifting from a Windows to a Mac operating system. It is picking up a soccer ball and dribbling it. It is an invitation rather than an imposition. It's an inflection point. It's a third way that creates an opening for something entirely new to emerge.

While there are countless ways you can shift the context, I've narrowed it down to four that are especially relevant for social change leaders:

- Shifting the context from entitlement to appreciation
- Shifting the context from concealing to revealing
- Shifting the context from vague agreements to healthy agreements
- Shifting the context from mediocrity to genius

I will teach you how to initiate all these context shifting moves in part IV.

When you learn to shift the context and initiate new structures and behaviors from your essence, you ripple out waves of transformation into the universe. You are literally creating a new reality. This is what taking healthy responsibility for the whole of the web of life looks like in action. And whether or not you succeed in your immediate aim, I can absolutely guarantee that by shifting the context you are opening up a whole new range of possibilities.

So that pretty much sums up the journey ahead. To recap, these are the things you are going to do:

- Face your challenges
- Embrace your power
- Clarify your commitment
- Shift your context

This is not for the fainthearted. Are you *sure* you are ready to do this? Good. Let's call in your support team.

Act Now: Gather the Energy of Everyone Who Is for You

Think about a time that you've taken a risk in your personal or professional life.

Think about the person or people in your life who supported that change. Did they give you a gentle hand up or a not-so-subtle push out of the nest? _____

_____

_____

_____

Maya Angelou poetically refers to these people who support you in this way as "rainbows in your clouds." I have witnessed people from Indigenous cultures refer to this process as seeking the permission of your ancestors. In the Buddhist Metta meditation, they are referred to as "benefactors."

So before we begin on this journey, in whatever way is most resonant with you, take a minute and reflect on whom the people are in your life whose love and presence will guide you along this journey. Then let's name names.

Write their names down here: _____

_____

_____

_____

_____

_____

Chapter 2 Takeaways

- Facing Your Challenges means being willing to be with reality as it is. Not how we want it to be, but what is real, right now. To start the facing process, ask yourself the following:

- Am I creating the change I want to create in the world?
- Am I living in a way that is aligned with my deepest values?
- Am I leading in a way that is true to my most authentic self?

- As you face your challenges, it is also important to explore the extent to which organizational toxicity or broader forces of societal oppression are at play.
- Embracing Your Power means a clear-eyed assessment of your societal power and positional power and a reclamation of the agency you forgo when you're on the Drama Triangle.
- You always get to choose whether or not to take action in any situation.
- Feeling your feelings creates an opening through which something new can emerge. Ask yourself:
    - Where am I out of alignment with my essence?
    - What have I not allowed myself to feel?
- Clarifying Your Commitment means tuning into your essence, that is, your deepest values and most authentic self. It is here where your commitment can emerge, and that will become your compass for what is next.
- Your ability to shift your context (from checkers to chess) is a very high leverage point.
- Shifting Your Context takes your internal commitment out into the world in a way that is most likely to effect change. While there are infinite

ways to shift your context, for the purposes of
this book we will focus on four of them:
- Shifting from entitlement to appreciation
- Shifting from concealing to revealing
- Shifting from vague agreements to healthy
  agreements
- Shifting from mediocrity to genius

CHAPTER 3

FACING TOXIC ORGANIZATIONAL DYNAMICS

While you may have an infinite number of challenges to face "out there" in the world, I want you to start with facing what is toxic in your team. We start here because I have yet to meet a social change leader whose organization is free from toxicity. So, it's good practice to get started on something meaty, with the added bonus that addressing these issues will create even more spaciousness so you can tackle the big uglies beyond the confines of your organization.

These are the most common organizational dynamics that I've seen sabotage change efforts within organizations, teams, and networks:

- Indecision
- Blame and criticism
- Micromanagement
- Overwork and overwhelm

When these dynamics are at play, they consume the mental and emotional bandwidth of everybody in range, leaving little energy for the genuinely difficult work of advancing social change. And what are organizations, really, other than groups of people presumably with some shared values and norms working toward a common objective? It's nothing but people and relationships.

Even though these dynamics can show up very differently from team to team, what they all have in common is an imbalance of power. For people to thrive in the work of repairing the world, these dynamics must be dismantled. They must be dismantled both in their most obvious manifestations (blame, criticism, overwork, overwhelm, indecision, and micromanagement) and also ultimately by going all the way down to their roots in a small group of people having power over others.

If you don't dismantle these dynamics, all the way down to the roots of oppression, you will waste your time stewing over them, and waste your precious energy on resentment.

But nothing happens until you face these issues and acknowledge they are real. In this chapter, I will invite you to explore the four major sources of organizational toxicity and assess the extent to which they are present for you and your teams. Let's start with perhaps the most obvious: indecision.

Indecision

I will share true stories of leaders facing challenges in each of these sections because I want you, the reader, to be able to relate. And honestly, I had difficulty picking just one example of a leader struggling with indecision because there are *so many* stories for me to choose from. I truly do not know where to begin. Here are some ways I've witnessed leaders bungle decision-making:

- Meetings where the facilitator solicits input, but the group fails to make a decision or communicate how or when a decision will be made
- Strategic planning retreats where the leader is reluctant to make decisions
- Meetings where the leader announces a decision without any process for including others
- Excruciating community meetings where the presumed need for consensus holds everyone hostage
- Emails where a decision is made, but it's so vaguely written that you're not sure if it implies that you personally should actually do anything

While it's difficult to find that Goldilocks "just right" way of approaching decisions, it's a worthy endeavor to liberate yourself as a leader and your colleagues to have much greater impact.

In the spirit of taking healthy responsibility for what matters to you, I want to suggest that one of your most important jobs as a leader is to make decisions. That said, you don't have to make all the decisions yourself. In fact, you shouldn't. Maybe a better way to say it is that your most important job is to *facilitate* decision-making.

Most of the time when you are leading a group of people or an organization, the best thing you can do is cede the decision-making power to others with thought and care. Take off that hero cape and invite others to the table to make and own the decision. Ideally, delegate decision-making authority to the people who will actually have to live with and implement those decisions.

You do not need to come up with the answer, only with how the answer will be attained. You must then state this clearly and equip the decision-makers with the information and resources they need to arrive at a sound decision. In the military, this is called the "commander's intent."

Once you've done all that, it is your responsibility to back the heck up. In the military, we called this the 3 Ds: Decide, Delegate, and Disappear.

This may seem counterintuitive, but if you are constantly trying to make all the decisions by yourself, you will buckle under the weight of that responsibility and you will deprive your colleagues of two things: (1) ownership over those decisions and (2) the developmental opportunity to build their own good judgment that comes with making (bad) decisions over time and learning from them.

So deciding by yourself should be off the table for you as a leader, except for in true emergencies.

The Latin root for the word "decide" is *decidere*. It literally means to cut off all other options. And sometimes making a decision can feel just like choosing to kill off all the other possibilities. It feels that way because, well, you are.

Some leaders are allergic to decision-making. Like me. I have an ENFP or Extroverted, Intuitive, Feeling, Perceiving personality type in the Myers-Briggs typology. The "P" (Perceiver) preference shows up for me in my love for being open to all the options and possibilities. I love being spontaneous. I am an option-and-possibility-creating machine. Want someone good to brainstorm with? Invite me over, give me an empty dry erase board, a handful of markers, and a glass of sun tea, and at some point, you'll have to ask me to go home because I will completely lose track of time.

But that comes with a downside. I don't like cutting off my options, which is exactly what decision-making requires.

I caution leaders not to over-rely on consensus as the primary method for arriving at decisions. Other than when we're clarifying our shared purpose, vision, values, and aims, it generally is best to avoid dragging everyone else through consensus hell.

As the leader, it is your responsibility to ensure that sound decisions are made in a timely manner. Period. And it's a really serious responsibility. Not all leaders have fully faced or reckoned with the gravity that entails. It could be as egregious as decision avoidance and hoping it will go away, but it can also be more subtle, such as when you don't feel confident enough to simply state, "OK, team, here's the challenge, and here's my request regarding how we will decide." It takes a certain confidence and awareness of your role to call the game.

If you yourself are indecisive, or if you work with or for someone else who is indecisive, you don't have to fix it all at once. As with the other toxic dynamics we're exploring, the first step is to notice that it is happening—those decisions are either not being made or are being made poorly, in your judgment. Indecision can have many causes, including the possibility that it's just not time yet to make a decision. But one of the biggest drivers of indecision is being in limbo. If you want to jump ahead, we explore limbo and commitment more deeply in chapter 7. For now, let's start by facing into the extent to which indecision is a challenge for you right now.

Act Now: Identify Your Indecision

Is indecision (yours or someone else's) a problem for you right now? _____

If you had a magic wand and could "poof!" the decision into being made, what specific things would you want to be decided? (Examples could be whether or not to enter into a strategic partnership, how much of a bonus to give employees, or what to do about a barrier to your team's progress.)

_____

_____

_____

_____

_____

_____

_____

_____

_____

_____

Once you've listed everything you can think of, reflect on your list, and circle the top two or three items that are causing you the most distress. Who is responsible for making those decisions? Is there anything you can do about them right away?

_____

_____

_____

_____

_____

On a scale of 1 to 10, how much is this draining energy from your work to change the world? (With 1 meaning "It's a rock in my emotional shoe" and 10 meaning "This is sucking the life out of me.")

$$1 - 2 - 3 - 4 - 5 - 6 - 7 - 8 - 9 - 10$$

Are you willing to support a decision being made?   **Yes / No**

Blame and Criticism

One of our fellows (who requested anonymity) shared a story that captures perfectly how widespread and insidious blame and criticism are in social change contexts. She was working for one of the largest and most well-known foundations in the US. She had a passion for making things happen, and yet, multiple times her boss pulled her aside and said, "You move too fast. Not everyone moves at your pace. You should be more realistic in terms of your expectations of people. You need to be more mindful of that."

Our fellow's heart sank. She interpreted her boss's criticisms to mean that she wasn't able to be her authentic self on this team. And she wondered, *Who is "everyone"?* And if this was the case, why weren't her peers saying this to her directly? She wondered if people were complaining about her behind her back.

You might be thinking, *What's wrong with giving somebody constructive criticism?* I would like to suggest that there is no such thing as "constructive" criticism. Criticism is always destructive.

The telltale sign that the communication above has blame or criticism in it is the use of "should." The word "should" indicates that someone is making a judgment. That's what our brains do—or at least one of the things our brains do—they make judgments. There's nothing wrong with judging. We cannot stop our brains from doing it. The problem arises when we wrongfully assume, as her boss did, that our point of view is correct. The problem is even worse when we're the boss or have identities that are privileged in our society. Unfortunately, having more positional or societal power often translates into having less humility and curiosity. When, as change leaders, we lose our humility and curiosity, we become part of the problem. Blame and criticism are one manifestation of that.

A culture of blame and criticism will eventually break people's spirits and rupture relationships. Eliminating blame and criticism from your life (both at home and at work) is an essential first step for creating the kind of world in which you want to live.

When my mentor Kathlyn Hendricks first introduced the possibility of eliminating blame and criticism from my own life, I thought, *No way is this possible.* I had a false belief that somehow blame and criticism were necessary tools for learning and growth. Now I realize that blame and criticism have zero transformational power. They do not help me or anyone else grow. They do nothing other than reinforce self-righteousness and force others into defensive reactions. They're antithetical to making the world a better place. They've got to go.

I should note that blame and criticism aren't reserved just for your colleagues. You might use them on yourself, too. Some people, like me, reflexively orient blame and criticism toward others. Other people, like my wife, tend to orient their blame and criticism inward.

Here are some variations on blame and criticism, both "outie" (directed toward others) and "innie" (directed to the self) style, that may sound familiar to you:

Outie	Innie
You should have done _____.	I should have done _____.
You should not have done _____.	I should not have done _____.
You always take all the credit.	I hog all the credit.
You never give me enough credit.	I never get enough credit.
You did it wrong.	I did it wrong.

I don't like _____ about you.	I don't like _____ about myself.
Why did you _____?	Why didn't I _____?
Maybe you're not the right person for this job.	Maybe I'm not the right person for this job.
I guess if I want it done right, I'll have to do it myself.	I'm not good enough.
Is that the best you can do?	Something's fundamentally wrong with me.

Blame and criticism are toxic and contagious, especially if they start at the top. Blame and criticism are effective and powerful ways of controlling others. Because shit rolls downhill and blame and criticism are basically that (shit), being on the receiving end is incredibly dangerous—especially when you have less positional power. And these toxic dynamics aren't just in organizations; they fester throughout sectors and systems as well.

In reality, blame and criticism are distractions. They distract you from what's really important, sow division, and keep you from the more important work of repairing the world.

But before we go any further, I want to differentiate blame and criticism from the similar but fundamentally different notions of feedback and critique. As a leader, it is essential that you are able to give feedback in a way that is entirely lacking in blame or criticism so that your colleagues can learn and grow. Equally important is your capacity to seek and receive feedback on the ways in which your decisions and actions are impacting others. Feedback is required for learning, growth, improvement, and transformation. Critique is an analysis of the power dynamics at play, and it's impossible to make any lasting change without a redistribution of power. It is possible to critique without blame or criticism and doing so increases the odds of your success.

What Is Feedback?

"Feedback" is giving another person the gift of revealing to them how you have experienced them. In its most simple form, it is vastly different from blame and criticism. Take a look:

Blame or criticism	Feedback
Your presentation sucked.	I lost track of what you meant somewhere around slide fifteen.
You made me angry.	I feel angry that you did that.
You are stupid.	I have some additional information I'd like you to consider.
You don't care.	I am concerned by your behavior.
You're selfish.	Your decision had an impact on me.

See the difference? When you're blaming or criticizing, you're attacking another person's being. When you're giving feedback, you take responsibility for your own experience and follow up with measurable actions that can be changed. There's no attack.

Imagine how different the opening scenario of this chapter would have been if my fellow's boss had said something like this: "I can tell you are deeply passionate about our work, and I respect you for that. And I noticed in that last meeting I found myself feeling protective of your peers, and then I wondered what the heck was going on for me. I noticed I felt that protective urge when you were pushing back on them about the implementation timeline. I'm making up the story (as in I am literally concocting a story in my head right now) that your expectations aren't realistic, and I am genuinely curious about what you were experiencing. Can you tell me more about what comes up for you in those moments?"

Again, see the difference? In the new example, the boss is noticing and sharing her own experiences (feeling protective of their colleagues, feeling curious about that feeling, her judgment that our fellow wasn't being realistic, and again curiosity about what the other person is noticing and experiencing). Nobody is being made to feel wrong. Nobody needs to waste any energy being defensive. Both parties can roll up their sleeves and dig into the work because they're still on the same team.

What Is Critique?

Critique is a critical skill for being able to see and dismantle oppression. But it is distinct and different from blame and criticism. Critique requires us to flatten any hierarchies or power imbalances.

Critique invites you to clearly face the presenting problem and inquire into the substrata of forces that kept the problem going. When you critique, you sit, as my colleague Joe McCannon likes to say, "on the same side of the table." Then, together, you harness the power of mutual curiosity to untangle the strands and come to a shared understanding of what's going on.

Infusing appreciation into everything you do is the antidote to an organizational culture of blame and criticism. If you want to jump ahead to explore appreciation further in chapter 8, go ahead and we'll be right here when you get back. Another option is to face the reality that blame and criticism have a seat at the table of your one and precious life and be with the discomfort it creates. That's what facing your challenge is all about—*being with* the discomfort—so you can fully feel those feelings and make a new choice from your essence.

Act Now: Blame and Criticism

Reflect for a minute on the extent to which blame and criticism are in your environment, then answer these questions:

Where in your life do you experience being blamed or criticized? _____

_____

_____

_____

_____

_____

Who in your life blames or criticizes you? Name names. _____

_____

_____

_____

_____

_____

What is their number-one complaint about you? _____

_____

_____

_____

_____

_____

Where in your life do you blame or criticize others? _____

_____

_____

_____

_____

_____

Who do you blame or criticize? Name names. _____

_____

_____

_____

_____

_____

What is your number-one complaint about them? _____

_____

_____

_____

_____

_____

What do you believe about blame and criticism? And who taught you that? _____

_____

_____

_____

_____

_____

On a scale of 1 to 10, how much are blame or criticism draining energy from your work to change the world? (With 1 meaning "Not at all" and 10 meaning "This is sucking the life out of me.")

$$1 - 2 - 3 - 4 - 5 - 6 - 7 - 8 - 9 - 10$$

Are you willing to create a context that is free of blame and criticism? **Yes / No**

Micromanagement

I personally have micromanaged and have been micromanaged several times throughout my working years. Whether I'm on the giving or the receiving end, my sense is that fear is the dominant emotion and trust is the missing currency. Here's a recent example from my own life.

When the COVID-19 pandemic hit, my company, the Billions Institute, had to pivot hard. Up until that point, 100 percent of our revenue was generated by live, in-person seminars. Within a month, my one full-time employee at the time and I began to transition all our seminars from live to virtual formats. This entailed a tremendous amount of additional content creation, project management, and coordination. There were many details to attend to, and details are not my strong point. I knew we needed something to keep us on track, and then I discovered Trello. Turns out Trello can be used to micromanage everyone and everything down to a gnat's ass: who will do exactly what, by when, and color coded! (Trello can also be used to optimize flexibility and flow, which is how we use it now, but that's another story for another time.)

In my panicked state, I went on a Trello bender. I micromanaged myself and my colleague to the point of absurdity. At one low point, I asked my colleague about the status of one particular task. She had no idea what I was talking about, so I explained in frustration, "But it's in the Trello!" In retrospect, this was truly embarrassing behavior as a leader, but at the time I was genuinely demoralizing myself and my colleague. My colleague gave me the feedback that perhaps I was going a bit overboard and I needed a vacation. This was a wakeup call for me, and I realized my personas had darn near overtaken my business. I was creating the conditions of micromanagement, overwork, and overwhelm.

I knew I had to shift my behavior, so I gave myself the time and space to get curious about what was going on inside myself. In my reflection, I realized I was feeling afraid and guilty at the same time. I was feeling afraid that I would not be able to provide for my own family, much less keep making payroll and retain this employee. I was afraid that people wouldn't want to attend our seminars virtually. I was afraid people wouldn't have money to afford any seminars in the first place. I was afraid that I'd never get everything done because my wife and I split our workdays in half to take turns caring for the kids. But way more than any of the above fears, I was afraid that I or my partner or our kids or someone else I loved would die a terrible death. I was grieving the massive suffering and loss that people were experiencing all over the world. At the same time, I felt guilty that we were able to insulate ourselves from the vast majority of risks by staying at home with our two young kids. It had nothing to do with Trello. Once I realized that I was feeling scared about so many things and had become a control freak in the process, I called my colleague, acknowledged what I was feeling, and apologized for my behavior. And luckily, she decided to give me and the company an opportunity to make things right.

It is your job as a leader to shift from the question "How can I get all these people to do what I want them to do?" to "How can I support all these people in doing what they want to do?"

I've found that anytime I'm micromanaging, I'm actually feeling scared of something I haven't quite articulated and do not trust the other person to fully understand. How can you have trust when you can't even articulate what you feel afraid of or what agreements you'd like to put in place?

When I experience being micromanaged, the story I make up is that the other person is afraid of something they're not telling me, and they do not trust me or my judgment. In those situations, I spend a lot of mental energy trying to anticipate what will please the other person and when that fails, I get defensive around any perceived negative feedback.

The bottom line is nobody wants to work for a control freak. Nobody wants to be a control freak, either. But most of us want to be in control. Hence, the dilemma.

The definition of management is "the process of dealing with or controlling things or people." The notion of control is built in to the very definition. Whether you're the micromanager or the micromanagee, you've probably been there. Without an intervention, micromanagement only tends to spiral and get worse until somebody quits or is fired.

People don't want or need to be controlled or manipulated. Micromanaging gives us the illusion that we are in control, but often it is just that—an illusion.

And yet, right now there are millions of people going to work every single day in the social change sector who, with the very best of intentions, believe it is their duty to control others, all under the guise of "good management."

There are also thousands of people going to work every single day dreading being micromanaged, second-guessing their own instincts, and looking over their shoulder to see whether or not the boss is pleased. They are afraid to bring their whole selves to the work. If you have an aspect of your identity that is marginalized in our society and have internalized that experience of marginalization consciously or unconsciously, then being micromanaged can further cause deep emotional wounds for you.

When micromanagement occurs, either party involved can request a pause to review agreements, those that are explicit and, perhaps more important, those that are implicit. But before you do that, you will want to sharpen your skills for speaking unarguably, which you can read more about in chapter 9, and check out discussion of healthy agreements in chapter 10. But for now all I want you to do is face into whether or not the dynamic of micromanagement has any place in your effort.

Act Now: Micromanagement

Who, if anyone, do you micromanage? Name names:

_____

_____

_____

_____

_____

What are the specific incidents or situations where you have believed you needed to micromanage someone? Do they have anything in common? _____

_____

_____

_____

_____

_____

What is your story about why you have to do this? I have to do this because . . . _____

_____

_____

_____

_____

_____

What are you scared will happen if you don't? _____

_____

_____

_____

_____

_____

_____

Who, if anyone, micromanages you? Name names: _____

_____

_____

_____

_____

_____

What are the specific incidents or situations where micromanagement occurred? _____

_____

_____

_____

_____

What is your story about why they do this? _____

_____

_____

_____

_____

What is holding you back from saying something? _____

_____

_____

_____

_____

On a scale of 1 to 10, how much is this draining energy from your work to change the world? (With 1 meaning "It's a rock in my emotional shoe" and 10 meaning "This is sucking the life out of me.")

$$1 - 2 - 3 - 4 - 5 - 6 - 7 - 8 - 9 - 10$$

Are you willing to create healthy agreements in your important relationships? **Yes / No**

Overwork and Overwhelm

Eunice Lin Nichols became the director and cochair of Encore.org's Gen2Gen campaign in 2016. This ambitious effort sought to mobilize a million adults aged fifty and older to stand up for, and with, young people so they can thrive. I know Eunice well, because she is one of our fellows. I know her campaign well because the Billions Institute consulted with Encore.org to help them design it. I met Eunice back when she was working part time and directing another program at Encore.org, their Purpose Prize. The Gen2Gen campaign had just about everything it needed—except a leader.

Although Eunice wasn't officially part of the campaign design team, she joined our planning retreats from time to time. Whenever she showed up, it was obvious that she was the ideal person to lead this campaign. Eventually, Encore.org's CEO, Marc Freedman, convinced Eunice to take the job, but not without some significant sacrifices on Eunice's part.

As Eunice tells it, she had not fully thought through all the ramifications of transitioning from a part-time job to a very full-time job, while still being the primary person managing the home front with two young kids. Eunice's commute time doubled because she now had to travel during San Francisco's rush hour. She brought work home with her and answered a never-ending stream of emails late into the night. She juggled a complex matrix of bargaining with other mothers to chauffeur her children to soccer practice and to pick them up from school when she was running late. And her family still depended upon her to cook dinner every single night. Eunice was deeply committed to the Gen2Gen campaign, but something had to give.

I am guessing that you might relate, on a daily basis, to what Eunice experienced. Our culture places such an unhelpful premium on the notion of "hard work." But it is focused, thoughtful, essence-paced, purposeful, creative contribution that is most likely to make lasting transformation.

While it may look admirable and heroic on the outside, agreeing to accept time scarcity as a construct or as a norm is actually counterproductive to the change we seek. In their book *Scarcity*, behavioral economist Sendhil Mullainathan and psychologist Eldar Shafir write about how we create the conditions for time scarcity when we believe we don't have enough time. Our bandwidth narrows and our capacity for creativity and doing our best work diminishes.

One of your most important jobs as a social change leader is to supply time and space; you can't give what you don't have. Overwork and overwhelm can be contagious, especially when the person who is overworking has positional power and generates an unsustainable amount of work for others in their wake. This is compounded by the fact that people have a deep need to belong. So if overworking is what it takes to fit in, more and more people will light the candle at both ends and burn that midnight oil. When you do that, you lose spaciousness and your ability to connect, and you sacrifice the creativity that comes from wondering and visioning, venturing out into the unknown.

It's very tempting and easy to blame people "out there" or "the organization" for your experience of overwhelm and over- work, and in many cases, there is some nugget of truth to that. But you still have a choice in how you participate in that. Or how you don't.

Here are some indicators you might be overworked or overwhelmed:

- Late to meetings more than three times in a month
- Double-booked or overlapping meetings
- Unprepared for anything you have committed to doing
- Always explaining why you can't possibly take on more responsibility
- Perpetually unable to complete your to-do list (if you keep one)
- Don't believe you can take some time off because you'll fall too far behind
- Feel the need to check your email while you're on a date (meaning you're overwhelmed or just plain rude)
- Allow work to routinely creep into your evenings, weekends, and vacations
- Feel everything is urgent and everything is a priority
- Experience a range of somatic symptoms and emotional signs like exhaustion, resentfulness, and irritability

A lot of people may think that the above list is normal, saying, "That's just the way things are, Becky. We live in the real world, and we just have to deal the best we can." The truth is that the "real world" can be overwhelming. It is also entirely possible that your organization is understaffed and under-resourced.

The closer you are to the pain people are experiencing, the more overwhelmed you might feel. It's one thing to be late turning in a report to a funder; it's another thing entirely to be less than fully present with a person who is dying, a student whose parents abuse them, a family being evicted, or a father being deported. The spiritual and emotional toll of overwhelm is on a continuum and will vary from person to person, day to day. It is real and I am not here to dismiss it in any way.

For now, your task is to face the fact that you are experiencing overwork or overwhelm (if indeed you are). There is no need to assign blame to anyone, including yourself. All you need to do right now is to face into what is true for you.

If you are operating in a context of overwork and overwhelm, the ultimate way out of this pattern will be proactively changing agreements. Let's take a moment to face the extent to which overwork or overwhelm are part of your life right now.

Act Now: Overwork and Overwhelm

Without any need to be perfect, accurate, or correct, take a minute to jot down all the ways that you personally experience overwork or overwhelm in your work to change the world. Some examples are working weekends and missing important family events. _____

_____

_____

_____

_____

_____

Once you've listed everything you can think of, reflect on your list and circle the top two or three items that are causing you the most distress.

On a scale of 1 to 10, how much is this draining energy from your work to transform the world? (With 1 meaning "It's a rock in my emotional shoe" and 10 meaning "This is sucking the life out of me.")

$$1-2-3-4-5-6-7-8-9-10$$

What is merely an annoyance to you? _____

_____

_____

What is sucking the life energy out of you? _____

_____

_____

Are you willing to create a new relationship with time and space? **Yes / No**

The Role of White Supremacy Culture in Toxic Organizational Dynamics

We've invested a fair amount of effort thus far into pinpointing exactly which oppressive dynamics are getting in the way of our work to repair the world. We've faced some of the most common and widespread organizational dysfunctions, including blame, criticism, the scarcity that fuels overwork and overwhelm, indecision, and micromanagement. All these dynamics take us away from making an impact in the world, but they do not occur in isolation. They are part of a broader dynamic, namely white supremacy culture.

I had been working with teams for years on improving their dynamics when my friends at the National Equity Project shared Tema Okun's original 1999 article on white supremacy culture with me. As I read it, I literally sat on the edge of my seat, enthusiastically highlighting and underlining words and phrases that resonated with me. The big realization for me was that these dysfunctional dynamics don't just come out of nowhere; they are deeply embedded in our notions of what is good and right and proper and professional, and these notions are deeply rooted in white supremacy culture.

Some white people shut down at the mention of white supremacy culture. If this is you, I encourage you to bring your curiosity and loving attention to your own resistance and bear with me because this is a biggie. While white supremacy includes people in organizations like the KKK, it's far more pervasive and insidious. It's based on the idea that lighter-skinned people are superior to darker-skinned people. This belief is what undergirds the systemic racism that has made its way into most institutions and into policy and practice in the United States. When we work in the United Kingdom, we often hear that racism isn't as much a problem there as classism. I would argue both racism and classism are relevant in the United States and in the United Kingdom. In chapter 5, I will ask you to explore more deeply your own societally constructed power (or lack thereof) that is due to race, class, and other factors, and what you can do about it.

White supremacy culture underlies all our organizational dysfunction, fuels our burnout, and prevents us from having the impact we want to have. Some of the hallmarks of white supremacy culture that our Billions Institute participants identify as most prevalent in their organizations are perfectionism, paternalism, fear of open conflict, overwork as the stated norm, and transactional goals and relationships. These dynamics are business as usual for many, so it's useful to know that you're not alone and that you didn't cause them in the first place. They have been used to divide and conquer, separating us from our bodies and one another for centuries if not millennia.

I implore you to read Tema's updated article "White Supremacy Culture—Still Here," which can be found at www .whitesupremacyculture.info. I believe her insights into the deeper and more pervasive roots of oppression deserve special attention. Tema pinpoints some of the more nuanced ways that toxic organizational dynamics can become an organizational staple, each with its own unique flavor or variation. She does a brilliant job of connecting the dots between something fairly obvious (workplace dysfunction) with something not as obvious to all of us (white supremacy culture). She lists antidotes as well, so it's not all doom and gloom. You can also hear Tema's thoughts on this directly from my interview with her in episode 18 of the podcast *Unleashing Social Change.*

Before we move on to embracing your power, let's do one more self-assessment of your organization's toxicity, incorporating some of the most prevalent aspects of white supremacy culture.

Act Now: Fully Facing Organizational Toxicity and Societal Forces of Oppression

Please take a moment to identify which issues, concerns, and problems on this list, some of which are drawn from Tema Okun's "White Supremacy Culture," are most present in your interpersonal and organizational contexts right now. Check as many as apply:

- ☐ Blame. I/we put energy (the amount is unimportant) into determining whose fault something is.
- ☐ Criticism. I/we look for things that are wrong and need fixing.
- ☐ Overworked. I/we routinely work outside normal work hours and feel exhausted.

- [ ] Overwhelmed. I/we don't have enough time.
- [ ] Unrealistic timelines. I/we set timelines that are not reasonable.
- [ ] Indecision. I/we don't make decisions in a timely manner.
- [ ] Micromanaging. I/we try to control what others do in a way that is overbearing.
- [ ] Being micromanaged. I/we are oriented toward pleasing the boss.
- [ ] Financial distress. I/we don't have enough money.
- [ ] Perfectionism. I/we can't make mistakes.
- [ ] Paternalism. I/we make decisions that impact others without fully involving them in the process.
- [ ] Fear of open conflict. I/we avoid challenging one another.
- [ ] Power hoarding. I/we withhold information, resources, or power from others.
- [ ] Transactional goals. I/we have superficial goals that fail to tap into our passion and purpose.
- [ ] Transactional relationships. I/we only reach out to others when I/we need something from them.
- [ ] Individualism. I/we believe I am/we are responsible for solving problems alone.
- [ ] Either/or thinking. I/we use good/bad, right/wrong, with us/against us thinking.
- [ ] Right to comfort. I/we believe that only those with power have a right to emotional and psychological comfort.

Please use this space to list any other toxic dynamics impacting your work that are not listed above: _____
_____
_____

_____

_____

Which of these toxic dynamics are most urgent and important for you to address now? _____

_____

_____

_____

_____

When you're finished, take a moment to appreciate yourself for being willing to face your challenges. Even though it might not feel great in the moment, it is progress!

Now that you've faced what is going on with you and/or your organization in the broader organizational and societal context of oppression, you don't get to skip right to nice, neat, tidy packaged solutions. There is no such thing. We will get to forging a new story of what is possible.

But first, it's time to get curious about how you personally are situated relative to these toxic dynamics.

The next step is absolutely essential, though it may make some of you feel uncomfortable.

It's time to embrace your power!

Chapter 3 Takeaways

- The first step in changing anything is in facing clearly what is actually happening.
- Four of the most common organizational dynamics that undermine social change are these:
  - Indecision

- Blame and criticism
- Micromanagement
- Overwork and overwhelm

- Leaders have a responsibility to decide how decisions will be made. You don't have to make every decision yourself. In fact, ideally, you shouldn't.
- It is possible to entirely eliminate blame and criticism not only from your organization but also from your life. If these are in your life, start by facing into that fact and then eliminate the word "should" from your vocabulary.
- Instead of asking "How can I get these people to do what I want them to do?" leaders can ask "How can I support these people in doing what they were put on this planet to do?"
- Overwork and overwhelm are rampant in social change work and will lead to burnout, but it doesn't have to be that way. Keep reading to explore your own responsibility in keeping these toxic dynamics going.
- All these toxic dynamics have their roots in centuries of domination and oppression.
- You can make big changes in the world, but until you face what is actually going on, history is destined to repeat itself.

PART II:
EMBRACE YOUR POWER

There are definitely problems "out there." I'm not disputing that for a second.

But this book is about you. And me. Not "them." That's the magic move.

Turn your attention inward and ask:

- How am I part of keeping this going?
- What would I like to do differently?

In this part, we turn our attention from what's going on "out there" in your change efforts, your organizations, and your society to "in here," to your own role in unconsciously keeping it going.

We will do a deeper dive into Karpman's Drama Triangle, which you read about earlier, and courageously face into your own unique patterns of subconsciously enabling the status quo.

Do you throw temporary fixes at the problem in "Hero"?

Or stand on the sidelines and point out what everyone else is doing wrong in "Villain"?

Or do you shrug your shoulders and say, "Nothing's ever going to change" in "Victim"?

Or, like me sometimes, do you cycle through all three in the course of an afternoon?

Finally, you will be facing into your relative power—or lack thereof—to address any given situation. You will start with your societal power that comes from the privileged or marginalized aspects of your multiple identities and consider how they will stack up. This is connected to centuries of societal oppression that none of us asked for but all of us were born into. Then, you will face into your positional power in your organizational contexts. Societal and positional power inform the risks associated with your range of options. We're going to be real about that. You will conclude this part by making a choice. Do you want to do something about the situation or not? And this choice is yours and yours alone. You don't have to do anything. And if you choose to do something, you will do so with your eyes wide open.

CHAPTER 4

OWN YOUR DRAMA

As long as you're entangled in any of the contexts that you faced into in the last chapter—indecision, blame, criticism, micromanagement, overwork, overwhelm, or any norms of white supremacy culture—you are hindered from making your big dent in the universe. This chapter will help you wake up and see your own role more clearly so you can then choose something different for yourself.

While it makes perfect sense to think that those toxic and oppressive dynamics are happening "out there" (and they are), the question you now have to ask is this: How am I consciously or unconsciously engaging "in here" with what is actually happening around me?

This is not to imply in any way that these oppressive dynamics are your fault. The idea here is to move beyond faultfinding entirely, starting with bringing your curiosity and attention to how you are unconsciously engaging with these dynamics and unwittingly keeping them going if you are on the Drama

Triangle. You can't change anything until you are aware of your own patterns and relationship to these dynamics.

Remember, this is the magic move, the shift from "out there" to "in here." If you do what I teach in this book, one person will change for sure, and that person is you. And we're all inextricably linked, right? So the changes in you will ripple out in all directions.

Let's proceed.

The Drama Triangle

To understand how you are unconsciously interacting with the oppressive contexts holding you back in your efforts to make change in the world, we need to know a bit more about the Drama Triangle, which you first read about in chapter 1. Let's explore it more deeply.

A quick refresher: The Drama Triangle is a social model of human interaction, originally developed in the 1960s by Dr. Stephen Karpman, a psychologist studying transactional analysis. He was analyzing fairy tales and noticed that every single one has a Victim (someone who needs rescuing), a Villain (the person causing the problem), and a Hero (the one who saves the day). This dynamic can be seen across all interpersonal relationships when things have gone awry.

Think about it. You've heard hundreds, maybe thousands, of stories in your lifetime that all contain a Victim, a Villain, and a Hero. Think about all the fairy tales you heard as a kid, all the books you've read, and all the movies and TV shows you've watched. Drama is everywhere. It is our metanarrative. And, you get the chance to wake up and choose something different.

This Victim/Villain/Hero notion has made its way into your psyche—so much so that you probably don't think about it. Seeing through the surface level of what is happening to the more basic building blocks of any societal, institutional, or interpersonal drama is an essential skill for being able to change the world and create something different from the same old same old. The Drama Triangle holds the key to understanding both how cultures function and how to subvert them.

Anytime you react to a given situation from an adrenalized state, you go onto the Drama Triangle. A sure sign that you're on the Drama Triangle is that it seems like a lot is happening without any real movement toward resolution. Energy is spent. Emotions run high. But in reality, all that bluster just keeps feeding the same game: the perpetuation of more drama.

The Drama Triangle versus Your Essence

The alternative to being on the Drama Triangle is choosing to respond from a grounded place of essence. You read about essence already, but to recap, "essence" is your most authentic self in an undisturbed state. It's the real you. When you react from a place on the Drama Triangle, you keep the current pattern going. But when you respond from your essence, you create new possibilities. Rather than reacting from a place of fear, you cultivate your capacity to respond.

The only way to effectively address the oppressive contexts that prevent effective social change is to do so from *off* the Triangle. And getting off the Drama Triangle starts with you.

As I mentioned before, the Drama Triangle is comprised of three personas. Like actors in a movie, these personas of Hero, Victim, and Villain are the roles we play. People form personas in childhood on occasions where just "being" is insufficient; they resort to "doing" to receive a caregiver's love and attention. And let me be absolutely clear about this: people need attention. It's not just nice to have; it is essential. Personas show up when you're feeling scared that you won't get the love and attention you need. This happens to all of us, me included. We all play each persona role at different times depending on the situation, but most of us have our favorites, the masks we wear that are most comfortable. We contrast personas with our essence, our natural, unperturbed state.

So let's take a deeper look at your fears and how you might manifest your place on the Triangle as the Hero, the Villain, or the Victim (or all three).

Let's start with the Hero. The hallmark of a Hero in an organizational setting is that they don't want anyone to be uncomfortable, so they run around solving problems for people. The challenge with this is that it diminishes other peoples' sense of agency and confidence. It's also a recipe for burnout for the Hero themselves. And it never really solves the overarching problem, because doing so would require uncomfortable conversations that Hero personas are quite allergic to having.

A Villain is always looking for who's to blame. They point fingers and find things to criticize. Their natural habitat is the water cooler, spreading gossip and talking behind peoples' backs. They generate a lot of drama but don't actually change the situation. They just create a bluster and get everyone upset.

The Victim has given up on being able to do anything about anything and has lost touch with their sense of agency and creativity. Victims believe the things that are happening to them are not at all the result of their own doing. Adopting the Victim persona is entirely different from being subject to actual victimization, such as being the victim of a crime.[3]

---

3. It is important to differentiate the Victim persona (an internal orientation of being at the effect of somebody or something else) from broader societal norms that oppress and extract from entire groups of people. It's also important to separate the experience of adopting that persona from the experience of being a victim of a crime, which is why we have chosen to capitalize it. We will explore this more deeply in the section on facing into your societal power, but there is absolutely nothing in the concept of the Victim that suggests you are to blame for your own oppression or

For now, let's bring the conversation back to how these personas show up in you as they relate to work. Remember:

The Victim says, "I *have to* work this weekend."

The Villain says, "I *should* work this weekend."

The Hero says, "Sign me up to work this weekend!"

Which persona are you embodying in your organization? Let's find out.

Act Now: Where Are You on the Drama Triangle?

Pick a challenge you are facing that you would like to explore further. Write it down here: _____

_____

_____

Reflect on your orientation toward that challenge. Are you more inclined to orient toward it from the Hero, Villain, or Victim position on the Drama Triangle? _____

_____

_____

On the next page you'll find a triangle with Hero, Villain, and Victim each in its own corner. Write in each corner of the triangle notes about times you have been each of these personas. Keep in mind these persona characteristics as you go:

- Hero: Takes more than 100 percent responsibility for the situation; sees others as less than whole;

---

crimes that have been perpetrated against you. Oppression is real. The Victim persona is more about how you orient yourself to that experience of oppression. You could be the victim of oppression or the victim of a crime and react to that experience from the point of view of the Victim, Villain, and/or Hero.

believes people need rescuing; looks for problems to be solved; and colludes with dependence narratives

- Villain: Takes less than 100 percent responsibility for the situation; looks for who or what to blame or criticize, including themselves; clings to fixed positions and indulges in self-righteousness
- Victim: Takes less than 100 percent responsibility for the situation; has lost their sense of agency and is at the effect of both the Villain who has caused the problem and the Hero, who may or may not show up

What are some of the perceived benefits for you of being on the Drama Triangle? What do you get as a result of taking on the Hero, Villain, or Victim persona? _____

_____

_____

_____

_____

_____

Likewise, what is it costing you to remain on the Drama Triangle? _____

_____

_____

_____

_____

_____

Why People Stay on the Drama Triangle

Drama can feel exhilarating. You get a rush of adrenaline that can make you feel like you've really accomplished something important. But operating this way is also physically and mentally exhausting. Physically, because our bodies are not designed to run on adrenaline for long periods of time, though our entire culture is addicted to it, and it is literally killing us. And mentally, because we start to see that, despite all our hard work, nothing of significance is really changing.

Many people spend a good portion of their lives on the Drama Triangle. Whenever you blame, criticize, offer unsolicited advice or assistance, or resign yourself to the idea that things will never change, you are on the Triangle.

You are on the Triangle anytime you look for who or what's wrong, including with yourself. You are on the Triangle anytime you micromanage. You are on the Triangle anytime you cannot make a decision but believe that you "should." You are on the Triangle anytime you are trying to operate while overwhelmed. You are in "reactive-brain" mode, which means the activity in the prefrontal cortex, the part of your brain used for higher thinking and reasoning, slows down, and your amygdala, the ancient part of your brain that is designed to respond to physical threat, lights up.

The short-term benefit of fueling your social change work from the Triangle is that you get the adrenaline hit and the satisfaction of believing you are right, regardless of whether you are in the Hero, Villain, or Victim position. You get to feel somehow better or superior to others, and that admittedly feels good in the short run. Unfortunately, that righteousness takes you out of relationship and connection, drags other people onto the Triangle with you, and the cycle of oppression is destined to continue.

The main point here is that the toxic dynamics happen *on* the Triangle. For example, in chapter 3 we covered some toxic workplace dynamics. Let's revisit them quickly through the lens of the Drama Triangle.

Blame and criticism fit squarely in the realm of the Villain. Villains avoid 100 percent of the responsibility for a situation by pointing their fingers. What Villains fail to do, however, is create loving pressure for change, which is what is required for lasting social change. The Villain blusters and obfuscates with blame and criticism, when what would be much more powerful is a clear, unequivocal, uncompromising no. Villains also fail to create a context of appreciation, which I like to think of as the train tracks on which all sustainable change rides.

Feeling overworked and overwhelmed is usually a blend of being the Hero and Victim. The Hero bites off more than they can chew in the first place and cannot bear for anyone to be uncomfortable. The Victim persona believes it is at the effect of people or forces outside itself. They are overwhelmed because they "have to" do all this work (that they agreed to do in the first place). The Victim "has to" do things, while a more empowered response is to *choose* to do things. There is a big difference between having to do something and choosing to do it. Meanwhile, the Hero persona overextends themselves, and never considers the possibility that perhaps the work as it is currently distributed is not sustainable. So the cycle repeats.

Micromanagement is usually a blend of Hero and Villain. The Hero takes more than 100 percent of the responsibility for the situation and gets all up in someone else's business with control tactics. The Villain avoids responsibility, judging the other person as somehow requiring micromanagement. The alternative is to see the other person as whole and fully responsible for their choices and action, while giving them room to make and learn from mistakes. See the difference?

Indecision is usually the realm of the Victim or a function of being stuck in a fear trance and a state of confusion. The Victim takes less than 100 percent of the responsibility for a decision being made, promoting indecision by deferring and allowing lack of clarity to persist. On the other hand, when you're in your essence, you recognize when a decision is required and bring people together to decide in an appropriate manner.

You can use the Drama Triangle to diagnose any cultural or organizational oppression, but even the most accurate diagnosis doesn't change anything. The name of the game is not to accurately diagnose where other people are on the Triangle, as you will be sorely tempted to do, but to notice when *you* are on it yourself, and then consciously choose something different. Now, let's unpack the three personas a bit more to look more deeply into your own patterns when it comes to the Drama Triangle.

The Hero Persona

Most of us who work in the social sector cherish the fact that we are doing something to make other people's lives better. Some of us even get called heroes. Remember the nightly clapping in cities around the world for all the health care workers during the COVID-19 pandemic? Unquestionably, there are people risking their lives for the sake of others, and they are true heroes.

What we're talking about here is a different version of Hero, which is why we capitalize it. The Hero persona rests on the belief that other people can't solve their own problems (an assumption many nonprofits make). This becomes an issue when you attempt to rescue people from something they may not even see as a problem. When you do this, you hit resistance because nobody wants you to solve their problems for them.

Fundamentally, people want to see themselves, and be seen by others, as having agency and dignity. This is the difference between doing charity work as opposed to justice work. Charity says, "Poor you, let me fix it." Justice stands in solidarity with people who can solve their own problems.

The Hero complex is related to false, but deeply imbedded, notions of white supremacy. A lot has been written about the problems of the white savior complex in the philanthropic and nonprofit sector. Briefly, the white savior complex refers to a white person who acts to help Black people, Indigenous people, and people of color in a self-serving manner.

A great example of this white savior complex and the problems with it on the macro level is the story about the white doctors attempting to address child malnutrition in Vietnam. They thought they had all the answers, but it was only when they got humble and curious that they realized some moms were adding baby shrimp and greens to the children's food and that was all the other families needed to do. The answers were already in the community. Once they realized that, they could get to work in solidarity with the community instead of parachuting in to rescue people.

In chapter 1, I wrote about inadvertently perpetuating the white savior complex in my *60 Minutes* interview. Unfortunately, this was not the first time. I was guilty of the white savior complex going all the way back to when I first started working on street homelessness. I wrongly assumed that the (mostly white) professionals who were doing street outreach had the right answers to address the problem of people sleeping outside in Times Square. I didn't have a racial justice lens at the time—I'm still working to have one now—and I definitely made up the story that I was the only thing standing between the people I met on the streets and utter misery. I believed that they somehow needed me and weren't capable of solving their own problems.

Fortunately, I noticed pretty quickly that an approach with roots in the white savior complex wasn't working, so I got humble and curious and sat down on those urine-stained streets of New York City for an entire summer and actually *asked* people what they wanted and then we actually *listened* to what they said. We designed the Street to Home Initiative around their answers and showed up in a stance that was much more about solidarity with people on the streets than about charity. We weren't there to hand out sandwiches or make their lives on the streets more comfortable; we were there to navigate the housing placement labyrinth alongside them, as their partners and their friends.

The white savior persona is just another manifestation of the Hero persona that is helping other people to alleviate the Hero's own suffering, rather than asking the people they intend to serve what they really want. The white savior persona, like all our Hero personas, can only offer Band-Aids,

when institutional and structural changes are what is required
to create real change.

If your organization's purpose is coming from the white
savior position, then your policies and procedures are likely to
be coming from a Hero persona, too. That will filter down and
affect your interpersonal relationships, especially with your
colleagues. So, what does the Hero persona look like within an
organization?

Hero-ing Your Colleagues

For many years, my primary orientation to my work was from
the Hero persona. I thought it was my job as a leader to literally
carry as much on my back as was humanly possible. I skipped
meals as I hurried from meeting to meeting. I got to the office
before dawn sometimes and left way after dusk. I stayed up late
at night responding to a never-ending stream of emails and
woke up each morning to more emails in my inbox. If a client
came in on a Friday night at 4:45 ready to go to detox, that
meant I would personally walk with them to the nearest hospital and stay with them until they were admitted, usually hours
later. If I didn't go with them and stay until they were admitted,
I knew the hospital would discharge them with some aspirin.
This happened way more often than you'd think. Whenever I
was given the opportunity to take on more responsibility in
the organization, I enthusiastically said, "Yes!" because that's
what I believed leaders do: take on ever-increasing amounts of
responsibility.

Eventually, this Hero mode of taking on more and more
responsibility put me on the path to burnout. I had taken on
more responsibility than I could handle, and my own scarcity
mentality blocked me from thinking I could hire more people

to help distribute the burden. I grew resentful and contemplated quitting on a daily basis.

But nobody was doing this *to* me. This was all of my own making. Luckily, I worked for someone who saw that I was burning out and one day over coffee asked me, "How can we free you up to do what you really love?" This one question yanked me out of my Hero persona and opened up the possibility that I might actually be more of service to the world by letting go of things that were burning me out. We will cover how you can do this, too, in chapter 11.

Keep in mind that self-imposed Hero-ing doesn't just come out of nowhere. It can be driven by those racially oppressive markers society imposes on us. Heather Kawamoto, race, equity, and social justice expert at Collective Liberation LLC, offered another angle on the Hero persona based on identity: Due to the internalization of white supremacy, many Black people, Indigenous people, and people of color receive a lot of messages throughout their lives about needing to work twice as hard and do twice the work. That doing so is what you have to do to survive working in a white dominant institution. That's just one way the Hero persona can be manifested and make you fight for survival.

Anytime you're in survival mode, your fight-or-flight response gets activated and you can fall into the Hero persona. I'm all about surviving; you have to do what you have to do. But, in addition to surviving, I want you to thrive. What that means, from my perspective, is all of us coming together to dismantle the structures and norms that perpetuate white dominant culture. It's not going to happen overnight, but we will know we're making progress when nobody has to tell their children "You have to work twice as hard and be twice as good" to get by in this world.

Shifting Out of the Hero Persona

This dismantling work and the unwinding of the Hero cannot be done by the Hero.

The Hero cannot bear for anyone to be uncomfortable and therefore twists themselves into a pretzel working overtime, or rushing into communities of color to save the day only to have the work backfire completely. But lasting change occurs when you allow yourself to feel authentic compassion while also holding firmly to the notion that communities and individuals are fully whole and fully capable of solving their own problems. By this, I do not mean "pull yourselves up by your bootstraps." You can't pull yourself up by your bootstraps if you don't have any boots. What I mean is showing unwavering solidarity. But first, you have to be humble and curious enough to ask if and how you might be able to be of service.

There is a world of difference between popping out of a cake with all the answers and standing shoulder to shoulder with someone and saying, "Gosh, this sucks. Is there anything I can do to help?" The former is classic Hero behavior; the latter is where you eventually want to go. So, how do you get there? Let's take a moment to explore if this Hero persona is coming to work with you.

Act Now: Hero Persona Assessment

Think about your issues. Which, if any, of these Hero moves are familiar in your life or in your work? Check as many as apply:

☐ Exhibiting the white savior complex: being a white person who acts to help nonwhite people, with the help in some contexts perceived as being self-serving

- [ ] Delivering Band-Aids instead of institutional and systemic solutions
- [ ] Providing charity rather than justice
- [ ] Taking on more than your fair share of responsibility
- [ ] Doing somebody else's work
- [ ] Being fearful of making anyone else feel uncomfortable
- [ ] Being unable to set a boundary or say no
- [ ] Saying yes to things you don't really want to do
- [ ] Agreeing to work nights or weekends when you don't really want to
- [ ] Withholding feedback from colleagues (because it would hurt their feelings)
- [ ] Looking for problems that need solving
- [ ] Wondering what people would do without you
- [ ] Giving unsolicited advice
- [ ] Designing programs for (rather than with) people
- [ ] Believing people need you and feeding dependency narratives
- [ ] Other: _____
  _____

How many did you check? _____

Circle the one that is most problematic for you and bring that into the next section of the book with you.

If you could give your Hero persona a name, what would you call them? For example, I call my Hero persona the Eager Beaver, as it is always running around trying to help people who didn't ask for help. _____

The Villain Persona

Anytime you catch yourself blaming or criticizing anyone, there's a good chance you're in a Villain persona. Villain personas are really good at pointing fingers, assigning blame, and declaring what's wrong. To be clear, the Villain isn't one in the traditional movie-villain sense; rather, they are constantly attempting to identify whom they believe to be the bad guy in any situation. They are in a Villain mindset, always. While it is never fun to be on the receiving end of someone's Villain persona, one thing that has helped me over the years is to remember that, no matter how prickly a Villain persona may appear, underneath this is someone who is simply afraid of something. It's no big deal if we can keep that in mind.

Villains are really good at diagnosing problems, but they are inept at doing anything productive about them. True solutions come from a grounded, adrenaline-free place off the Drama Triangle.

At the societal and political level, our metanarrative is locked in a never-ending Villain-off. Both sides of the issue are often busy trying to convince the masses that it's the other side's fault. Whatever the problem is, it's "their" fault. This paradigm is so pervasive in our society right now that it can almost seem normal, but I assure you it is not. It is toxic. Your work as a change agent starts with extricating yourself from this dominant paradigm. I can rant and rave with the best of them, and for a few minutes it actually feels good. But my rants don't change anything.

What to Do About Your Villain Persona

Lurking underneath the Villain persona is often an unexpressed no. By this I mean your essence registers an authentic no in response to the situation, but for whatever reason you may not be willing or able to express your no in that moment. For example, you might have an authentic no to anything, from something as small and simple as another serving of cake to something as vast and complex as capitalism or racism. One of the best ways to interrupt the Villain persona is to get curious about what you might have a no to and express that directly from your essence instead of indirectly from your Villain persona.

There's a big difference between wagging fingers and standing firmly in the place of "no more," and holding that energy until the injustice is addressed or the broken boundary is restored. The key is holding yourself in that place until things are made right, which takes a lot of courage and persistence. Anybody can complain. Social change leaders don't just complain; we stay in relationship with the necessary people to make things right.

I wish I had learned this lesson much earlier in my life than I did. In the early days of the 100,000 Homes Campaign, I spent a lot of time in my Villain persona. There was one relatively powerful person who I thought was subverting our efforts. In public, they professed to be committed to tackling homelessness in the region, but I knew that behind closed doors they were riding the brakes.

I spent a lot of mental energy complaining about her and trying to figure out how we could work around her subterfuge. Rarely did I complain to her face, mind you. Mostly I would gossip about her behind her back to my colleagues, and we would commiserate with one another about how awful she was. Nothing creative or productive resulted from my complaining, blaming her, or gossip other than the short-term hit of adrenaline from believing I was right and better than her.

I wish back then I understood the difference between being in that Villain space of pointing fingers and blaming somebody else and asking, "Are you willing to cut this behavior out now?" I don't know what would have happened if I had challenged her directly, but I suspect it would be better than being her frenemy for a couple of years until she was rotated into a new job where I didn't have to interact with her anymore. Note the lingering Victim talk there with "have to." Nobody is immune to the Drama Triangle, including me.

Think of all the creative energy I wasted by complaining behind her back. Think of all the personal power I left off the table. And imagine what she might have done if I had calmly asked, "Are you willing to stop this now?" Can you see how my Villain persona was inadvertently keeping the oppressive environment going? Even though if you had asked me then I would have insisted that it was the other person's fault, the truth is I was keeping it going, too.

What responsibility are you avoiding? What leadership move are you delaying by staying in the Villain position on the Triangle?

Shifting from Villain to Challenger

Nothing good will result from showing up in your Villain persona. But how can you shift out of it and back into your essence?

One of the most helpful ways I've found to shift out of my Villain persona is to go back to basics. What am I feeling afraid of? Was there a violation of something I hold dear? What is it that I value the most, and how can I cultivate that in my own sphere without getting distracted by something in the distance? For me, the route out of my Villain persona is to turn my attention inward and get curious about what I really want, and then love myself for wanting that. In so doing, I give myself permission to want what I want. Sometimes there is an unexpressed judgment or request that I haven't made, and when I am willing to own it as such, the need to blame or criticize others disappears.

The assessment below will help you determine the extent to which your Villain persona is coming to work with you.

Act Now: Villain Persona Assessment

Here are some common variations of the Villain persona. Check all that apply to you:

- [ ] Blaming another person for what happened
- [ ] Blaming yourself for what happened
- [ ] Blaming an entire group of people for what happened
- [ ] Looking for things that are wrong
- [ ] Believing you're better than someone else
- [ ] Believing you're worse than someone else
- [ ] Believing your group is better than another group
- [ ] Believing your group is worse than another group
- [ ] Making reality wrong by clinging to how something "should" be
- [ ] Talking about anybody who is not present (in other words, gossiping)
- [ ] Rebelling by breaking the rules or cheating
- [ ] Justifying your bad behavior
- [ ] Attacking the messenger
- [ ] Attacking someone's character or essence
- [ ] Explaining how the other person didn't understand
- [ ] Employing any passive-aggressive tactic
- [ ] Other: _____

How many did you check? _____

Circle the one that is most problematic for you and bring that into the next section of the book with you.

If you could give your Villain persona a name, what would you call them? Here are a couple of examples to get your creativity going: Roller Derby Queen, Double-Down Dan, Take No Prisoners Tammy. I call my Villain persona Judge Judy. You get the idea. Have fun with this. _____

_____

The Victim Persona

The Victim persona believes they are at the effect of something outside their own control and are resigned to feeling sorry for themselves. Anytime you use the words "have to" to describe your choices or actions, it is a linguistic giveaway that you're in a Victim persona. The Victim believes things will never change and that there's nothing to be done about it. If the Victim persona were a gesture, it'd be a shrug.

When you are in the Victim persona, you lose your sense of agency entirely. For example, when I am deep in the grip of my Victim persona, I don't even know what I really want. It's so impossible for me to imagine I could have what I want that I don't even allow myself to conceive of it. You know you are in Victim mode when you have forgotten that you, too, have agency and that you can identify and ask for what you really want at any time.

Victim personas trade the power of their agency for attention. They abdicate responsibility for their situation to the Villain and hope a Hero will rescue them. In this way, though, a Victim persona can act helpless while in actuality they are dragging everyone onto the Drama Triangle with them.

At work, the Victim persona unconsciously colludes to keep oppressive contexts going. To the Victim persona, it appears as if everything is happening "out there," but the Victim persona is also enabling the drama to continue. The key is to catch yourself doing that and make a new choice!

When I first started exploring personas in my own life, I swore up and down that I didn't even have a Victim persona. Victim personas were for wimps! Well, it turns out my Victim was running the entire show. When I'm under stress, I tend to start with my Hero persona, and then when that doesn't work, my fallback is my Villain persona, which throws an elbow or two. When none of that works (and trust me, it never does), my Victim persona finally kicks into gear. Sometimes it's so pervasive that I feel trapped in an immobilized cage where I don't even know my own thoughts. I just feel so stuck. I can't imagine any other options and can't even think of what to do to get myself free. You will have your own patterns, but rest assured we all have personas and they come to work with us and sabotage our best plans!

I want to emphasize again that it is important to differentiate the Victim persona from two things: (1) broader societal norms that victimize entire groups of people, and (2) being a victim of a crime. These forms of victimization happen every single minute of every single day whether they show up as racism, sexism, homophobia, ableism, xenophobia, or any other host of traumas. We will explore this maldistribution of power more in chapter 5. Suffice it to say for now that oppression is not OK, but it happens, and it's not your fault. What I mean by Victim persona in this case is your inner orientation to anything that happens to you, including being on the receiving end of oppression. So I want to be crystal clear: societal oppression is not OK. *And* you still get to choose how you orient yourself to that phenomenon.

Shifting from Victim to Creator

Let me give you a specific example that is personal to me. My wife wanted to do a home birth for our first child. She was in labor for sixty hours at home, at which point we realized she needed to go to the hospital. An hour or two later, our son, Huck, entered the world through an emergency C-section. We received absolutely superb care from the hospital. Mama and baby were both healthy. We were elated and exhausted.

Then they brought us the paperwork for the birth certificate, which only had lines labeled "Mother" and "Father."

"But Huck has two mommies," we protested.

"Sorry, this is the only form we have," they said.

In that moment, my heart sank. I felt sad and even a little bit ashamed that maybe there was something wrong with our family because we are different. This internalization of shame and inferiority (in my case related to my sexual orientation and my family's composition) is what I'm talking about when I say that it is possible to be a victim of some form of oppression but not orient to it from a Victim persona. The concept of heteronormativity, the idea that heterosexuality is the default mode of sexual orientation, leads to the belief that a couple should consist of a man and a woman. And I was feeling the weight of that default binary in the hospital room. It's safe to say in that moment—and in many others like it based on one aspect of my identity that is marginalized in our society—I was a victim of homophobia and heteronormativity.

And being a victim of a larger oppressive force is entirely different from inhabiting the Victim persona, which is more about my inner orientation and *reaction* to what happened.

If in that moment I had said to myself, "There's nothing we can do about it; it's just the way things are here," I would have been taking on the Victim persona in response to an incident of homophobia. But that's not what we did.

Instead, my wife and I spoke about it, we felt our feelings of sadness and disappointment and shame. And we decided that while we were in the hospital, we would seek out the supervisor who would have the authority to change the form, which we did. And she did. So while I was listed as "Father" on Huck's birth certificate, two years later when my wife gave birth to our daughter at the same hospital, I was listed as "Parent" on Vivian's birth certificate.

Here's another example, where I experienced homophobia but stayed on the Triangle in a Victim persona. A couple of years ago, my wife and I met an old friend at a restaurant in Orange County, outside Disneyland. We were enjoying our meal when another couple caught my eye because they were literally glaring at us. We weren't being excessively loud. But this couple kept glaring at us in a really hostile way. My immediate assumption was they were offended by my gender expression—that I looked "too gay" or shouldn't be holding hands with my wife. I instantaneously ran through a bunch of scenarios in my head. Should I say something to them? Maybe say something snarky about them clearly not being from liberal California? Maybe provoke them with "What are you looking at, Buster?"

As I contemplated those scenarios, I also had the thought that the guy, who was wearing a cowboy hat and glaring at us, might have a gun. And he might shoot us or do something violent. So instead of challenging them, or asking them to stop staring at us, I asked for our check, and we left the restaurant. I felt scared for our safety, and the smartest thing I could come up with at the time was to simply leave. I was in survival mode. I may have been on the receiving end of homophobia, but I'll never know for sure. Maybe he had indigestion. But I definitely acted by instinct rather than from a place of thoughtful choice. And that's OK, too.

The antidote to the Victim persona is to find your way back to your essence, which has full access to your creative powers in all situations so you can make choices aligned with your whole and best self. Remember that, no matter what happens in life, you always have control over two things: your choices and your actions. You have the capacity to take healthy responsibility for anything and everything that is occurring in your life, even if what is happening is oppression and victimization. By healthy responsibility I don't mean that you should take the blame for anything and everything that is occurring. I mean that you can retain your agency and maintain conscious control over your decisions and actions, no matter what anybody else is doing.

The big question here is this: Are you unconsciously reacting or are you choosing to respond to the world around you? One keeps the drama going, the other holds the possibility for true transformation. Let's look at how the Victim persona shows up in your life.

Act Now: Victim Persona Assessment

Here are some common ways that Victim personas show up. Check all that feel familiar to you:

- ☐ Biting your tongue and not saying anything (because it won't make a difference anyway)
- ☐ Losing your initiative (because the boss will micromanage you anyway)
- ☐ Complaining about how things are and how they'll never change

- [ ] Failing to make a decision or even know that one needs to be made
- [ ] Inability to discern what you really want
- [ ] Inability to differentiate between your yeses and nos
- [ ] Explaining how it isn't your fault
- [ ] Saying yes to things you don't really want to do
- [ ] Inability to make clear agreements
- [ ] Inability to keep agreements
- [ ] Inability to hold others accountable for agreements
- [ ] Biting off more than you can chew
- [ ] Overpromising and underdelivering
- [ ] Hesitancy to occupy your full range of influence
- [ ] Remaining silent about things that harm you
- [ ] Not confronting others who are harming you
- [ ] Waiting for someone else to rescue you or save the day

How many did you check? _____

Circle the one that is most problematic for you and bring that into the next section of the book with you.

If you could give your Victim persona a name, what would you call them? Here are some examples to get your creativity going. I call my Victim persona Angry Penguin. Angry Penguin waddles around the house and passive-aggressively does the dishes and takes out the trash because "nobody else does" and because "at least I can control *something*." Some other fun Victim persona names might be Helpless Harry, Boo Hoo Sue, or Pity Party Pam. You get the idea. _____

_____

What to Do with Your Personas

Remember: personas are masks you learned to put on to survive. Even though they go about it somewhat messily, they are mechanisms you've created to protect you from harm and pain. So the first thing to do is to acknowledge and appreciate them. They have kept you safe and alive. Thank you, personas! I'm still here! Well done!

Personas are all about helping us survive, but unfortunately, they are no help whatsoever in helping us *thrive*. And they're definitely counterproductive for creating sustainable social change. So what do we do with them?

First, don't try to send your personas packing. When I first learned about personas, I thought they were flaws—faulty parts of me that I needed to shed. Even though I was explicitly told that is absolutely not the case (much like I am telling you right now), I still believed that something was fundamentally wrong with me for having these personas in the first place. And that makes sense. Once you begin to see more clearly how pervasive your personas are and how fantastically they mess things up, you may want to send yours packing, too. The problem is you can't actually get rid of them. But you can learn how to put them to work in service of your growth as a person, which will make you much more effective in your attempts to change the world. Catching yourself in a persona is not a problem, it's an *opportunity* and an *invitation* back to your essence, to your true self.

Your Victim, Villain, and Hero personas are just parts of you doing the best they can to help you when you're scared. But when you're in the grip of them, it's like having a three-year-old at the helm. Personas are parts of you coming up to the surface of your consciousness to be seen and loved. It is in welcoming and integrating these dissociated parts of yourself that your own healing begins. This journey starts with facing into what is happening like you're doing in this section of the book—both facing into what is happening "out there" in the world, and how you react to it "in here."

It can also be helpful to recognize your persona patterns. As I noted earlier, I found that when I'm stressed I cycle through all three personas on the Drama Triangle, but it took some reflection to see this. It's important to notice when you're on it. That way, you can take proactive measures to get off the Drama Triangle and back into your essence so you can be creative and form authentic connections with other people.

Three Techniques to Shift from Persona to Essence

When I realize I'm in one of my personas, I use one of three techniques that I learned from Kathlyn Hendricks to bring myself back into my essence.

The first is called "magnification" or, as I like to think of it, "make it bigger!" How it works is that I notice I'm in a persona and, instead of fighting it, I go all in and allow myself to wallow in it until, inevitably, it becomes comical. If not for anyone else in my life, at least it's funny to me. As soon as I catch myself laughing at how ridiculous I'm acting, I know I've broken the spell of that particular persona. I'll be honest: this technique is my favorite shortcut to snap out of it and back into my essence.

The second technique I learned is to actually interview my persona. To ask it a series of questions with the intention of discovering what this persona is really up to. There is a very specific way to conduct a Persona Interview that I learned from the Hendricks Institute. If you'd like to try this out for yourself, you may want to first watch me demonstrate it on our website, www.billionsinstitute.com/persona-interview. You can find the questions in appendix B.

The third technique is to use catching myself in persona as a cue that perhaps I am having some feelings about something, and allow my curiosity to sink into thinking, "I wonder what I'm not allowing myself to feel?" That's such a reliable method that we've devoted an entire chapter of the book to help you master the basics of it. If you can't wait to try this out, jump ahead to chapter 6.

For now, let's tune in to some of the constructed aspects of your power, societal and positional, on the way to grounding yourself in your personal power.

Chapter 4 Takeaways

- The first step to embracing your power is to ask how you may be unconsciously perpetuating whatever it is that you want to change.
- Karpman's Drama Triangle provides a quick diagnostic for the primary ways people keep a drama going: Hero, Villain, and Victim.
- Heroes believe that people need rescuing and cannot bear for anyone to experience discomfort. The problem with the Hero is that we all need some discomfort to change or grow. The Hero's own discomfort with discomfort can keep that change or growth from occurring.
- Villains avoid taking responsibility for the situation by focusing on blame and criticism. They get a hit of righteous indignation or self-loathing, but they don't actually create loving pressure for change. In this way, they're contributing to keeping the situation going, even if they are certain whose fault it is!

- Victims have lost touch with their inner sense of agency and believe someone else must rescue them for the situation to improve. They, too, keep the situation going, absolutely convinced there's nothing they could do about it.
- These personas get activated when you believe your survival is under threat. Unfortunately, your survival mechanisms are perhaps a little overdeveloped. You can go from Hero to Villain to Victim in the span of an afternoon. None of which succeeds in actually making anything better.
- Making sustainable, lasting change is only possible from your essence.
- While there are several methods for reliably getting off the Drama Triangle, in this book we will focus on feeling your feelings.

CHAPTER 5

OWN YOUR POWER

Remember, this book is all about repairing the world and breaking through any barriers to doing so. So far, you've made an initial pass at identifying the issues you want to explore. Next, you examined the extent to which organizational or societal contexts of oppression are at play. Then you opened up to the possibility and the ways that you are unconsciously and unwittingly keeping it going when you go on the Drama Triangle. And now, here we are with one final piece of that onion to peel, and that is your own relative power, and therefore risk, in any given context.

In this chapter, we will interrogate how you are situated relative to three different types of power: societal power, positional power, and your personal power to make a choice. Societal power is the relative advantage or disadvantage society confers on you due to aspects of your identity. Positional power is where you are in the chain of command relative to others. Personal power is the agency you choose to access at any given moment.

All three forms of power matter. All three are always in play. And while you always have control over the choices you make and actions you take, which choices are available to you are shaped by these broader constructs related to power. I wish power were equally distributed in our society. Until we create the conditions of true equality, the risk involved in making waves is unequally distributed. We would be foolish not to consider this before moving into the next steps.

Keep in mind that power and how you react to it are deeply tied to existing power structures built around race, gender, and class. To put it in the simplest terms, if you are a high-status white man reading this, as you face into whatever is holding you back from repairing the world, you may notice that you feel angry about that. And I should note that a clean expression of anger can be a powerful force for transformation. It belongs on the menu for all social change agents. And yet, there is almost zero risk in our society for you, as a white man, to simply express your anger. You might lose some status for expressing sadness, but anger for you is totally fair game.

If, on the other hand, you are a Black person of any gender reading this, as you face into an experience of injustice, and you notice that you feel angry about something, I don't have to tell you that the risk is higher for you than for a white male to express anger in our society. The clean expression of anger is still a powerful force for transformation, but the risks of you expressing your anger can literally be a matter of life and death.

Who gets to feel and say and do what, and who is constrained, is informed by a complex kaleidoscope of strategies our overall white dominant culture employs to hold its power. Our identities are rich and complex. Very rarely is it the case that someone is 100 percent oppressed 100 percent of the time. Likewise, many of us have aspects of our identities that are privileged by our society, while others are marginalized. Even more complex, some of us have identities that are oppressed in one context but privileged in another.

In this chapter, my invitation is for you to consider your own relative societal and positional power and do a thoughtful risk assessment as you choose how you will tap into your personal power. Let's start peeling that onion together.

Societal Power

The societal domain of power has been constructed over thousands of years. A person's level of power can be visualized as a multidimensional continuum. Each of us has more power in some domains and less in others. In any given interaction, some combination of these power dynamics is at play between our identity and that of others. Bringing awareness to this is essential for making conscious decisions about what you're willing to do to make change.

You can start the work of facing into your societal power by facing into the ideas and ideologies that are underneath our culture. One of our fellows, Michelle Molitor, founder of The Equity Lab, along with her colleagues Caroline Hill at 228 Accelerator and Christine Ortiz at Equity Meets Design, published a Medium.com article listing the 10 (+1) big ideas that fuel oppression in the United States.[4] For readers who do not live in the United States, I invite you to consider the extent to which these same or similar ideas have permeated your society as well.

With their permission, I'm sharing the 10 (+1) ideas below. As you read them, I invite you to stay curious about the extent to which they match your own understanding of how societal power is (mal)distributed.

---

4. https://medium.com/equity-design/the-big-10-1-ideas-that-fuel
    -oppression-97d7200929f9

- Idea 1: Lighter-skinned people deserve more love, power, affection, wealth, grace, and dignity than darker-skinned people.
- Idea 2: Men are smarter, more trustworthy, better leaders, more responsible, stronger, and more honest than women.
- Idea 3: Richer people are smarter, more trustworthy, and more responsible, and deserve more aspiration and grace, than poorer people.
- Idea 4: Christians are more trustworthy, righteous, and more justified in their violence than non-Christians.
- Idea 5: Heterosexuals are more natural and deserving of love, dignity, humanity, and companionship than lesbians, gays, and bisexuals.
- Idea 6: Cisgender people are more natural and deserving of love, companionship, dignity, and humanity than transgender people.
- Idea 7: English speakers with dominant-culture accents are more intelligent than non-English speakers or those with different accents.
- Idea 8: People who are differently abled (physically and mentally) are less intelligent than able-bodied people.
- Idea 9: Young adults are seen as smarter, more creative, more energetic, and more employable than older adults, teens, and children.
- Idea 10: Adults with college degrees are smarter than adults without college degrees.
- +1: The Stability Clause—The stability clause is perhaps the most dangerous of these ideas. It asserts that these ideas will not change and will continue to govern our relationships in the present and for future generations. The stability clause

is guilty of the most imperfect crime—the theft of power, agency, and hope.

These ideas permeate our culture and our consciousness. The question now is how does this metanarrative impact you personally?

This list is a really great springboard for thinking about your own power and how it affects your approach to leading social change. Here's how I applied it to my own experience.

Going down this list, I am a white, gender-nonbinary person married to a woman. We are well off financially. I consider myself a nontheist but very spiritual person. I am an English-speaking, able-bodied, middle-aged person with a master's degree living in the United States.

Some of these aspects of my identity confer unearned advantage and privilege in my context: my whiteness, my financial status, my command of the English language, my able-bodiedness, my middle-agedness (although that soon will veer off into "old"), and my master's degree. The advantage is unearned, but it exists, nonetheless.

My whiteness enabled me to grow up in neighborhoods that were relatively free from policing. Where I grew up, we never even saw a police officer because the belief was "there is no crime here," which simply was not true. It also enabled my family to buy homes in neighborhoods in which the public schools received sufficient funding.

Through my whiteness I accumulated decades of lies that I am somehow better than people of other races. I don't believe that consciously for one second, but sometimes my subconscious does. It has also made it easier for me to get jobs and easier for me to be perceived as successful in those jobs.

My privilege due to age and education make it much more likely that people will seriously consider my ideas. That has contributed to my family having plenty of money for everything we need and want to do. Our financial privilege enables us to buy our way out of most things that might cause discomfort. Don't like the public school our kids go to? *"Let's look at private school for next year."* Don't want to breathe too much pollution? *"Let's move somewhere else or get a really fancy air filter."* On a regular basis, my whiteness and my financial privilege open doors to people and places I might not otherwise have access to.

My privilege also makes it less likely that I will second-guess my choices or my actions. My privilege also lowers my risk threshold for doing many of the things I encourage you to do in this book.

There are also areas in my life where my privilege is a liability. For example, my privilege has reinforced a sense of individualism in me that is unsustainable and exhausting. My privilege has literally separated me from my own humanity. The dissociation I learned as a white person in particular has resulted in me having to work extra hard to be able to reconnect with my own body sensations and emotions so that I can tap into that wisdom to do the work I'm here to do in this lifetime. My privilege has made me have to work that much harder to form deep and lasting bonds with people who have different identities from me.

Although for me personally the decks are stacked toward privilege, there are contexts where I experience less societal power, primarily due to my identity as a gay and gender-nonconforming person. I didn't even consciously realize until a few months ago, in my fiftieth year of being on this planet, that I identify as gender nonconforming. As a kid I felt proud to be called a tomboy. I wanted nothing to do with dolls or things that were labeled "girl toys." I was literally kicked out of Blue Birds (a girls' club similar to Girl Scouts) for being so disruptive because I thought girl things as socially constructed were "stupid." I refused to wear a dress, with one notable exception:

prom. When I see pictures of me wearing my pink prom dress, my only question is, "Whose idea was it for me to go to prom in drag?" But the gender-binary trope is so powerful in our society that, until I turned fifty, I never even considered that maybe I didn't think of myself as fully boy or girl, man or woman.

How is that possible? And what did I lose of myself along the way?

Likewise, my identity as a gay person has resulted in my experience of marginalization. Though we gays are quite trendy these days, homophobia is alive and well and even a justification for murder in many places around the world.

When it comes to aspects of my identity that are marginalized, my experience is the converse of that from the areas of my identity where I have privilege. Instead of not questioning my choices and my decisions, I second-guess my decisions, my actions, and my worthiness to be at the table to make change in the first place. My risk in taking action goes up. Here are some ways I second-guess myself:

- Will people dislike or judge me if I wear this (really cool) men's sweater?
- Is it OK for me to cut my hair *this* short?
- If my wife and I hold hands in public, will someone try to harm us?
- If we fly a gay pride flag at home, are we making ourselves a target?
- Was that person rude to me because I'm gender nonconforming or holding hands with my wife, or are they just having a bad day?

The primary driver of my choices and actions is an unconscious but existential fear that puts me in survival mode. When I'm in survival mode, it's hard to come up with an answer. And my bandwidth is consumed by ensuring that I am safe and can survive. This takes me further out of full presence and my ability to connect with others. It is something I've been navigating since I was about five years old. I have had to work through my own internalization of the gender binary and heteronormativity. I'm not done doing that work, by the way. There are always more layers of that onion for me to peel as I reclaim my own wholeness.

In this context, I might wisely determine that making waves is a risk I'm not willing to take. At least not every single time. I might be more careful in my choices. Or I might be sure to bring my friends with me.

On the bright side, my own experiences of marginalization around gender identity and sexual orientation have given me the superpower of being able to quickly sense when a person or environment feels safe (or not). My experience of marginalization due to these aspects of my identity gives me a glimpse into how that might be for others, even though I will never fully know what any other person's experiences are. It opens up for me the possibility of being able to show up in solidarity with anyone who has been marginalized in any way, though it is not a given.

No matter whether it's a help or a hindrance, it's important for all of us to remember that our societal power is not static, even though it *seems* like it is fixed in stone. Yes, those 10 (+1) ideas that fuel oppression are real, but only because we've made them so. Even if we consciously repudiate these ten ideas, they've infiltrated our subconscious and that's what counts. But we can be part of changing them.

When I choose to take action, I do so with my eyes wide open. I encourage you to do the same.

Acknowledging the broader context of oppression that shapes our culture all the way down to and including our own internalization of it allows you to move forward to create new contexts of love and liberation.

The walls of the societal power structure are real, and they shape our options. Dismantling those walls is part of what many of us are here to do with our lives. Changing oppressive norms, rules, structures, and systems one interpersonal interaction at a time *is* the work. Now it's your turn to explore the way societal constructs shape your experience of marginalization or privilege.

Act Now: Face Your Societal Power

For each identity group (age, race, skin color, etc.) reflect on the extent to which you experience related privilege or marginalization. It might be different depending on what context you happen to be in. Then complete the journal questions below.

PRIVILEGED GROUP		MARGINALIZED GROUP
Late 30s to 50s/ early 60s	1. Age	Younger; older
White	2. Race	Person of color; people who identify as biracial/ multiracial
Male	3. Sex Assigned at Birth	Female; intersex
Cisgender	4. Gender Identity	Transgender; gender nonconforming; gender queer; androgynous
President; vice presidents; deans; chairs; directors; supervisors	5. Hierarchical Level	Direct service staff; "back office" staff
Heterosexual	6. Sexual Orientation	Gay; lesbian; bisexual; queer; questioning

Upper class; upper middle class; middle class	7. Social Class	Working class; living in poverty
Graduate or 4-year degree; highly valued school; private school	8. Educational Level; Credential; Certificate	High school degree; 1st generation to college; less valued school; public school
Christian (Protestant; Catholic)	9. Religion/ Spirituality	Muslim; Jewish; Agnostic; Hindu; Atheist; Buddhist; Spiritual; LDS; Jehovah's Witness; Pagan . . .
U.S. born	10. National Origin	"Foreign born;" born in a country other than the U.S.
Not disabled	11. Disability Status	People with a physical, mental, emotional and/ or learning disability; people living with AIDS/HIV+
"American;" Western European heritage	12. Ethnicity/ Culture	Puerto Rican; Navajo; Mexican; Nigerian; Chinese; Iranian; Russian; Jewish . . .
Fit society's image of attractive, beautiful, handsome, athletic . . .	13. Size; Appearance; Athleticism	Perceived by others as too fat, tall, short, unattractive, not athletic . . .
Proficient in the use of "Standard" English	14. English Proficiency	Use of "non-standard" English dialects; have an "accent"
Legally married in a heterosexual relationship	15. Marital Status	Single; divorced; widowed; same sex partnership; unmarried heterosexual partnership . . .

Parent of children born within a 2-parent heterosexual marriage	**16. Parental Status**	Unmarried parent; do not have children; non-residential parent; LGBTQ parent . . .
More years	**17. Years of Experience**	New; little experience
U.S. citizen	**18. Immigration Status**	People who do not have U.S. citizenship, are undocumented
Suburban; valued region of U.S.	**19. Geographic Region**	Rural; some urban areas; less valued region
Light skin; European/ Caucasian features	**20. Skin Color; Phenotype**	Darker skin; African, Asian, Aboriginal features . . .
Nuclear family with 2 parents in a heterosexual relationship	**21. Family Status**	Blended family; single-parent household; grandparents raising grandchildren; foster family . . .
Extrovert; task-oriented; analytical; linear thinker	**22. Work Style**	Introvert; process-oriented; creative; circular thinker

This list is used with permission of the Social Justice Training Institute. You can learn more about the institute at www.sjti.org.

"Cisgender" refers to gender identity or expression matching the sex assigned at birth while "transgender" refers to gender identity or expression not matching the sex assigned at birth.

Think about a specific situation in your work for change or your personal life where you experienced marginalization. Jot down not only what happened but also what body sensations you remember, what you were feeling, and what stories you told yourself about what that experience meant about you and the world: _____

_____

_____

_____

_____

_____

_____

_____

_____

_____

With respect to areas where you experience marginalization, reflect on the additional efforts required to keep yourself safe, whole, and in a space where you can keep doing the work.

_____

_____

_____

_____

_____

_____

_____

_____

_____

Now think about a specific situation in your work for change or your personal life where you experienced privilege. Jot down not only what happened but also what body sensations you remember, what you were feeling, and what stories you told yourself about what that experience meant about you and the world: _____

_____

_____

_____

_____

_____

_____

_____

_____

With respect to areas where you experience privilege, how can you lean into your humanity to take even greater risks for the whole of the web of life? _____

_____

_____

_____

_____

_____

_____

_____

_____

_____

What can you learn from each of these spaces (where you are privileged and where you are marginalized) to inform the other, in turn making yourself whole and leading with agency in all spaces? _____

_____

_____

_____

_____

_____

_____

_____

_____

_____

Positional Power

While societal power follows us around wherever we go, 24/7, positional power is limited to the workplace. This is where a lot of work for change happens (or doesn't). The question to ask is this: Who, literally, has the authority to do what with/for/ to whom? This is hierarchy in action. This is positional power.

There is nothing inherently wrong with hierarchy. It's natural (think queen bees and wolf packs) and can be useful for organizing groups of people toward the achievement of shared objectives.

Similar to power in the societal domain, our positional power might seem etched in stone. We may think it just is what it is. It is the dominant story of our lives, but that is not the truth. It is both stipulated and fluid, defined and beyond your direct control, but at the same time mutable.

It's also important to note that societal power plays a huge role in determining who winds up having positional power. People with identities that are privileged are more likely to wield positional power in organizations, too. You can't change the fact that power or hierarchy exists, but you can challenge and reckon with it no matter where you fall in the pecking order (I guess chickens have a hierarchy, too).

No matter what your positional power is, you can enhance your agency. Everyone is called to show up as a leader. The bottom line is everybody reports to somebody, and that somebody might be you. CEOs report to board chairs and board chairs have fiduciary obligations to the government, which reports to the citizens. If anybody neglects to perform their duties, they can be removed from power.

Ideally, accountability goes in both directions—up *and* down. The chain of command is strengthened by a sense of shared purpose and by knowing that our fates are intertwined. Unfortunately, in some organizations mutual accountability is replaced with a more oppressive might-makes-right-because-I-said-so way of operating. When people within an organization lose their sense of interdependence with one another, or never had it in the first place, their positions in the pecking order take on an even bigger meaning and can keep worthwhile voices from being heard.

Reckoning with Positional Power

When I was a graduate student at The New School, I did a fairly exhaustive study of all the different models of leadership. The one that seemed to hold the most weight at the time was this: teams are needed to get anything meaningful done in the world, and it doesn't matter *who* the team leader is, so long as there is one. So if you think of your positional power as a way of being of service to those on your team, you're headed in the right direction.

Sometimes, you might be reluctant to claim your power. But a leader's ambivalence or avoidance of stepping into the authority conferred by their positional power can be just as problematic as being overly authoritarian. Maybe you don't want to be overbearing, or maybe you worked under someone who abused their power and don't want to be like that. Maybe you are second-guessing yourself because of some aspect of your identity that is marginalized in our society. However, denying your own positional power can take you right to the Victim persona on the Drama Triangle, creating problems such as indecision and wasted effort.

I've found that my liberal or progressive-leaning friends can be especially reluctant to claim their positional power, as if somehow authority itself is bad. It's not. We had a saying in the army: "When in charge, take charge!" I want more social change leaders to take that to heart. When you are entrusted with authority, you have the opportunity—dare I say, the responsibility—to use that authority to advance healing, justice, and transformation. So take charge!

If you're ambivalent about being a leader, my question for you is this: In terms of the change you seek in the world, how can you use every ounce of your positional power in service of what matters?

Get aligned from head to toe with your power and how you intend to use it in service of what you are committed to. When you have positional power, your job is not holding people accountable; rather it is establishing meaningful partnerships and providing material support toward achieving a shared goal. My former boss Rosanne Haggerty once told me in a supervision meeting, "Consider me your secret weapon." She was inviting me to bring her in to break through barriers as needed, and she was really good at doing that. So much so that my team affectionately referred to her as the "R-bomb." As in, "Don't make us call in the R-bomb on this one."

Here are some other productive ways to envision how you might leverage or employ your authority:

- Make sure everyone understands the tasks ahead of them.
- Prioritize and coordinate across related efforts.
- Secure resources to remove scarcity conditions.
- Allocate resources so everyone has what they need.
- Notice when a decision needs to be made and decide how it will get made.
- Tend to the well-being of the people on your teams.

When you use your authority in these ways, you can direct your positional power in service of the change you seek, and you enter into a relationship of mutual accountability. That is the goal.

A Special Note to Philanthropists and People Working in Philanthropy

If you've made it to the point where you are redistributing your own or other people's resources in a significant way, your experiences, beliefs, and worldview will set the context that others will need to fit themselves into to access your resources. It is all too easy to slip into paternalism.

Here are a few things you can do in addition to deep and ongoing inner work to keep it real and be of service when it comes to philanthropic positional power:

- Acknowledge your role in perpetuating the problem you seek to solve.
- Focus on root causes versus Band-Aid solutions.
- Commit to funding long term and sustainably.
- Offer grantees support to remove barriers and obstacles.
- Create meaningful mutual accountability.
- Cede power to others, including grantees.
- Use your influence to get other high-net-worth individuals to do the same.

Here are some admirable examples from some philanthropic organizations I've worked with:

The Raikes Foundation, a philanthropic entity created by retired Microsoft executives Jeff and Tricia Raikes, gave a pool of money to a youth board that delegates to the young people experiencing homelessness themselves the authority to decide where the money goes.

In the **Building Equitable Learning Environments Network** designed by one of our fellows, Lindsay Hill, each grantee had to answer these questions: Which is the population you serve least well? And how do you need to evolve internally to better serve the constituencies you intend to impact? The grantees received three years of reliable general operating funding to participate in an authentic learning community with other grantees. Instead of issuing the standard request for proposal (RFP), the Raikes Foundation issued a request for learning (RFL). This groundbreaking network engages the funders as learners, too.

Emerson Collective, founded by Laurene Powell Jobs, uses philanthropy, impact investing, advocacy, and community engagement as tools to spur change. Sarah Rahman, their chief of staff for social innovation, shared that they have thought long and hard about how to level the power dynamic that exists within philanthropy and have built most of their practices with this in mind. The Collective focuses on making multiyear general operating grants and providing optional capacity-building support. Like the Raikes Foundation, Emerson Collective believes that the leaders they support know what's best for their organizations, and general operating support enables those leaders to use funds where they believe them most useful. This enables leaders to focus on the work itself instead of constantly fundraising every year.

The Einhorn Collaborative writes the annual grant summaries for their grantees so the grantee can hear what the foundation has learned and gotten out of their work and relationship. Imagine if instead of having to write an essay to justify your activities over the past year, the foundation wrote the summary *for* you to show you what they've learned from you. More of that, please!

Soon after the COVID-19 pandemic struck, the **Eisner Foundation** announced that all their grants were being restructured to be general operating grants and that no reporting would be required. Many others followed their lead.

Social Justice Partners Los Angeles, led by my wife, Christine Margiotta, has taken extensive measures to flip the script on funding social justice leaders directly impacted by the systems they're working to dismantle. Christine and her colleagues realized their grant application had fifty-two questions and was placing an unnecessary burden on applicants. They did away with a written application and instead created a workshop where all applicants could benefit from free training, learn from one another, and build relationships, even if they weren't selected for the program and funding. Social Justice Partners Los Angeles also shifted their annual pitch night from one in which nonprofits compete against one another for prize funds to one in which the nonprofits all share the collective text-to-give investments of the live audience. This is a great example of ceding power that also acknowledges the deep interconnectedness of social justice work.

There is a growing movement to decolonize philanthropy. If this is an area you want to explore more deeply, I highly recommend reading *Decolonizing Wealth* by Edgar Villanueva.

Act Now: Positional Power

Draw a basic org chart that shows where you are in the chain of command. Who reports to you and to whom do you report?

Circle all the people who are involved in any way in the challenge you're facing.

If you have more positional power than the others involved, how can you invite others to sit on the same side of the table as you? _____

_____

_____

_____

_____

If you have less positional power than the others involved, how can you lean into your personal power to punch above your weight? _____

_____

_____

_____

_____

Personal Power

Here is *the* paradox those of us who wake up each day to make the world a better place need to reckon with: no matter how ambitious our plans are for doing good in the world, at the end of the day, as Sharon Salzberg wisely says, all any of us truly has is our three feet of influence. In other words, we can only influence those in our immediate orbit, even when we're leading large-scale change.

The real question, regardless of your societal power or your positional power, is how are you going to use your *personal* power?

Everybody gets three feet of influence, no matter what. How will you use your three feet of influence to repair the world without breaking yourself? How will you use your three feet of influence to link up with other people's three feet of influence, too? You don't have to do this alone. In fact, if you want to succeed, you can't do it alone.

Consider your relative societal and positional power with regard to the issue you're facing. On the whole, do you perceive yourself as having more or less power than the person or people who are entangled in any ongoing drama with you?

If You Have Less Power

On the one hand, that's unfortunate because power can come in handy. On the other hand, you probably have more power than you think, and the rest of this book will help you get clear on how you want to use it.

First and foremost, though, I want to acknowledge that not having power is especially problematic in a culture that places such a high value on the individual (versus the collective). Your relative lack of power will require you to be resourceful, to collaborate, and to be incredibly creative.

It would be foolish and misleading for me to encourage you to throw caution to the wind and spread your wings and fly, baby, fly! I am well aware (because I've been there myself) that your reputation, self-esteem, and livelihood could be at stake if you speak up and attempt to change your circumstances.

So here are three suggestions for how you might tap into your personal power when you find yourself in a situation where you have less societal or positional power:

1. **Initiate small "safe-to-fail" tests.** Read all the recommendations in this book and try something that is small and safe to fail. By this I mean something so small that, if it doesn't go well, the harm to you or others is likely to be negligible. It could be something so simple as asking someone, "Are you open to feedback on my experience of that?" and waiting for the yes or no response. It could be saying one thing that is unarguably true for you and observing the effect your microreveal has on your context. Use that small safe-to-fail test to assess how open or closed to transformation the people in your context really are. You can also use small safe-to-fail tests to assess your own openness to

change. If it goes well, try another one, see how it goes, and over time perhaps you will grow bolder in asserting a new paradigm.

2. **Move on.** Sometimes your greatest power is in saying no. If you have been running into brick walls, are beyond the brink of burnout, and nobody else seems to share your concerns, update your profile on LinkedIn, find another job, and give adequate notice. Nobody said you have to stay in a toxic or oppressive organization. Maybe, knowing what you now know, you can find a better match. Quitting isn't a failure if it frees you up to take more responsibility for what matters to you in an environment that is more conducive to your well-being. If you don't have the financial freedom to quit right now, and you really feel stuck, then . . .

3. **Organize.** You are not alone. Maybe there are others who share your ideas about what could be done to make your organization much more likely to transform the world without you having to lose yourself. Find allies. The key is to *do this without gossiping, blaming, or criticizing.* Don't hang out at the water cooler and complain your face off. Apply the principles in this book to your organizing work. Keep reading to learn ways to do this that are off the Drama Triangle and from your essence.

If You Have More Relative Power

Great! Now your challenge is to fully own and occupy your power for good. What are you waiting for? What is your story about why you haven't already used the relative power you have to create the change you want to see?

If you feel cautious about being overbearing, especially if you have a significant societal or positional power differential with others involved, one thing you might want to reflect on is what resources—including power—you are willing to redistribute or give up.

Power is always about resources, which can be tangible or intangible. Tangible resources in an organizational context include money, staff, space, technology, and equipment. Intangible resources are just as, if not more, important. To get you thinking, here's a short list of intangible resources you can redistribute:

- Time: How much time is someone given to complete a project?
- Time: How much vacation time is allocated?
- Time: How long does someone get to talk during the meeting?
- Inclusion: Who gets invited to the team/meeting/decision?
- Attention: Whose voice is heard?
- Information: What is transparent and what is kept secret?
- Authority: Who gets to say no?
- Authority: Who gets to change their mind at the last minute?
- Authority: Who gets to show up late to the meeting?

If you are in a position of having more societal and/or positional power, and you want to create a life-giving and sustainable organization, it is worth the effort to face into how tangible and intangible resources are distributed and get to the work of redistributing them.

Make a Choice

Now it is time for you to choose what, if anything, you want to say or do about your issue using your various types of power. But first, ask whether you want to act at all. *Sometimes the answer is no.*

If you choose to do something about your challenge, you have the thrill of stepping into the unknown and seeing where it takes you. Choosing not to say or do anything is also a choice. And it's just as valid. Just remember you don't *have to* do anything about the issue you face.

There are four questions to ask when choosing whether or not to take action in any given situation:

1. What will you regret if you choose not to say or do something?
2. What opportunity might you miss if you choose not to say or do something?
3. What is the worst that could happen if you choose to say or do something?
4. What opportunities become possible with choosing to say or do something?

If those four questions are too complicated or take you down a pro-and-con-list rabbit hole, try substituting this one question instead: *Will doing something increase my aliveness?*

Even if your palms get sweaty. Even if you feel scared. Ask yourself what you can do in this situation that will make you feel even more alive. Taking everything into consideration, each choice is up to you. But you will want to decide at some point. When you feel ready, this is where a clear-eyed balancing of the risks and rewards is required.

Choosing to take action will inevitably increase your personal power in any situation, even if you are rebuffed. Here is why: you *chose* to *respond*. Even if you don't get the desired result, you are building your agency muscles, like working out in the gym. While your societal and positional power are less easy to change, by stepping off the Drama Triangle and introducing something new—an appreciation, a reveal, a request, a new agreement (something from your essence)—you are playing a different game. The more you practice showing up, the less power the Drama Triangle, or anybody who is on it for that matter, has over you.

If you decide *not* to respond to a situation, not necessarily because you're scared (although that may be the case), but because you've decided that it's simply not worth the risk, you will also increase your personal power because you are in control. If you choose not to respond, there is nothing to feel ashamed or guilty about. You have faced your issue, and that is a big deal. A lot of people go through life in the fog and confusion of the Drama Triangle and never fully face anything. When you get clear on what you really want and fine-tune your commitment, this sets powerful forces in motion, even without immediate action on your part.

And don't worry about doing this wrong. If you decide to take a pass for whatever reason, and this is something that's meant to be, the universe will find a way to give you a do-over.

While I want to encourage you to be mindful of risks, especially given how they are maldistributed in our society, I want to caution you about getting too caught up in your rational mind and invite you to also include in your calculus the wisdom your body is communicating to you. We will explore this further in the next chapter, but for now tune in to what generates the greatest feelings of aliveness for you. How do you notice your own aliveness? Is it the swelling of your chest as you open up to a possibility? Is it the tingling of your fingers? Is it the pulsing of your heartbeat that you feel in your body? Is it the sinking of your breath deeper into your belly that is your sign that this is right for you? Whatever it is, that's what I encourage you to listen to, even if it's a whisper right now.

Act Now: Do You Really Want to *Do* Anything?

One of my professors from West Point, Jane Holl Lute, went on to become deputy secretary general of peacekeeping for the United Nations. She is brilliant at simplifying and navigating exceedingly complex dilemmas. Over dinner one night she explained her "opportunity and regret index" to me. She said, "For every choice you make there's an opportunity index and a regret index. You just have to figure out which one is bigger."

Taking Jane's advice to heart, and bearing in mind that it's a perfectly valid choice not to *do* anything at all, reflect on your challenge and respond to these journal prompts:

If you choose not to say or do something, what will you regret most? _____

_____

_____

_____

If you choose not to say or do something, what opportunity might you miss? _____

_____

_____

_____

If you choose to say or do something, what is the worst that could happen? _____

_____

_____

_____

_____

If you choose to say or do something, what opportunity might
open up for you? _____

_____

_____

_____

_____

What would you choose purely for the sake of your own
aliveness? _____

_____

_____

_____

_____

Chapter 5 Takeaways

- There are three kinds of power: societal, positional, and personal.
- Societal power is unevenly distributed and therefore the risk of taking action is also unevenly distributed.
- Each of us embodies a complex web of identities, and it's likely that some aspects of your identity are privileged in our society while others are marginalized.
- Positional power can also impact your risk from introducing change and can be leveraged to create conditions of mutual accountability.

- While societal and positional power may appear to be fixed, they can both be impacted by people using their personal power.
- Everybody gets three feet of influence. Nobody can take it away from you and nobody can tell you how to use it. That is yours and yours alone to decide. We hope this book will help you use it wisely.
- You don't *have to* do anything.
- Whether or not you say or do something is your choice and yours alone.
- Consider the impact on your own aliveness. Tune in to your body wisdom for clues.
- Consider the risks involved.
- What's it going to be? Pass or play?

PART III:
CLARIFY YOUR COMMITMENT

I'll never forget my experience of fully committing to my work on homelessness. It was 1:00 a.m. and there was still plenty of traffic in New York City's Times Square. I was so excited I couldn't sleep, so I decided to drive my Subaru Forester past every single block in my new territory: from Twenty-Third Street to Fifty-Ninth Street, and everything from Sixth Avenue west to the Hudson River. Earlier that same day, Rosanne Haggerty had hired me to reduce street homelessness by two-thirds in three years in West Midtown. I wanted to see with my own eyes what I had gotten myself into.

With each passing block, I felt more weight of responsibility on my shoulders. Somewhere along the way, I lost count of how many people were bedded down for the night alongside dumpsters or in alcoves. Mind you, I had zero experience with street homelessness. Zero. But that didn't stop me from internalizing a sense of responsibility for everything I saw, because I also had zero ambivalence about my new job. In fact, I can now say with confidence that my entire being was aligned with this new possibility. I was fully committed.

That's the full-body experience of alignment I want you to take into any challenge you decide to tackle. You have made some real progress to get to this point in the process of working on your interior self to impact what's outside it. You've faced the problems that are holding you back from repairing the world without breaking yourself. You've faced into the ways you habitually orient to the challenges life brings you. You've grappled with societal, positional, and personal power. You have chosen whether or not to do something about your challenge.

Now it is time to clarify your commitment.

In this part, we start with helping you access the mental clarity that always comes on the other side of allowing yourself to fully feel your feelings. Then we will clear up any wobbles you still have about what it is you say you want. I will help you understand limbo, and then we will move on to three concrete skills you can apply to get yourself out of it: knowing your yeses, knowing your nos, and the power of commitment.

You will leave this part of the book with your commitment in hand. That way, when you begin the work of shifting your context in the final section, you will do so in a way that is deeply grounded in your own truth. When you are fully aligned with your commitment, you become a force to be reckoned with. No matter what anyone else says or does, you are clear about where you're headed.

You will start by feeling your feelings. Stay with me, Goose.

CHAPTER 6

FEELING YOUR FEELINGS AS AN ACT OF SUBVERSION

I know, I know. Feeling your feelings is the *last* thing you want to do. But I promise you, if you don't bring your body to work with you (and have reliable access to the wisdom it and your emotions are giving to you), you are only operating with a fraction of your capabilities.

Remember: leadership is a full-body sport. Injustice thrives when people repress their feelings and disconnect from their bodies. Feeling your feelings and learning to use them as fuel to create what you want is actually quite rebellious and subversive. Feeling your feelings (or at least not trying to push them away or cover them up) is what creates the space for something new and different to emerge.

Before I learned about emotional and body intelligence, I had two categories of feelings: good and bad. My body was trying to communicate with me, but I didn't know how to interpret what it was saying. We often develop a confusing and adversarial relationship to our emotions as children. I know I'm not alone in having been told, "If you keep crying, I'll give you a reason to cry!" when I was a kid. Or "Don't be scared; there's nothing to be afraid of." The problem is you can't talk anybody (including yourself) out of feeling afraid.

Maybe only one person was allowed to be angry in your home growing up, and it wasn't you! Many of us who are drawn to the work of repairing the world learned early in our lives that some feelings were acceptable (joy), and others were not (fear, anger, sadness, or sexual feelings).

Now I know that when I feel scared, it's simply my body trying to keep me alive (even when the risk may be imaginary). So I don't try to talk myself out of it. I know that is futile. And I definitely don't make any major decisions when I'm feeling scared. I simply breathe and move until I don't feel scared anymore.

When I feel sad, I allow myself to cry until those waves of sadness subside.

When I feel angry, I give a good "Grrr," shake my fists in the air, and say, "I feel angry."

When I feel sexual feelings or joy, I allow myself to enjoy it.

Unfortunately, many organizations send a very clear signal to employees that they are expected to be "professional." And by "professional" they mean 100 percent rational all the time, and utterly lacking in any emotional intelligence or expression. To realize your full potential as a change leader, you must ditch the toxic notion of professionalism that asks you to dissociate from your authentic experiences, and reclaim the rich and wise gifts of your body wisdom and emotional intelligence. It's not that rational intelligence is unimportant; rather, it alone is insufficient and incomplete for the work of repairing the world.

In healthy organizations (and relationships), people state clearly when they're feeling scared, because that's actually important information for others.

In healthy organizations (and relationships), people cry when they feel sad because it's a natural response to loss. (And given what's going on in the world, couldn't we all use some tissues?)

In healthy organizations (and relationships), people let others know when they feel angry. Anger is the proper response when an injustice has occurred or a boundary has been crossed. Dr. Julia Colwell likes to say that anger lets you know you aren't getting something you want or are getting something you don't want. I don't mean that you should kick the garbage can across the room and scream at somebody. That's abusive. I mean listen to your body—that clenching of your jaw, that pain in your shoulder—and calmly (as if you were asking someone to pass the salt over dinner) say, "Oh, I just noticed that I feel angry."

In healthy organizations (and relationships), the revealing and expressing of emotions, including sexual feelings and joy, is greeted with curiosity. That's the dream. These are the kinds of organizations (and relationships) I want to help you create.

You might be very familiar with your emotional landscape and the kaleidoscope of feelings that flow through you from day to day, minute to minute. If that's the case, good on you! But you may be uncomfortable thinking about what you feel. Maybe you've experienced a significant trauma and become dissociated from your body or emotions. Maybe you have been conditioned to believe your body and feelings are irrational, untrustworthy, and dangerous. Nothing could be further from the truth.

A huge swath of wisdom and intelligence is begging for you to pay attention. If the idea of feelings makes you uncomfortable, know that you are not alone. I want to encourage you to push yourself out of your comfort zone just enough to see if maybe there's something here for you.

In this chapter, we will explore some of the most common feelings that arise when you're leading social change: fear,

anger, sadness, sexual feelings, and joy, with a special emphasis on fear since that is the number-one saboteur of progress.
You'll have the opportunity to explore the emotions that arise
for you related to the challenge you identified in part I of this
book. And we will present several different exercises to help
you understand that mental clarity comes on the other side of
feeling them. Then we will take that mental clarity of knowing
what you want to the next chapter and form a commitment.
Making a commitment is the single most powerful thing you
can do as a change leader. I'll walk you through the steps of
doing just that, too.

I should warn you, though. Having trained thousands of
social change leaders, I can tell you that exploring emotional
terrain brings up some discomfort for a fair number of people.
So please bear with me if this discussion makes you uncomfortable. You might think I'm joking when I implore you to
bring your body to work with you, but I'm convinced that
doing so is perhaps one of the most important things you can
do in service of your work to repair the world.

I appreciate you for being willing to do this inner work.
Buckle your seat belts. Here we go!

Why People Don't Feel Their Feelings

To maintain a context of oppression, whether it's racism, sexism, colonialism, homophobia, ableism, ageism, xenophobia,
or any other ism, people need to be dissociated from their bodies. When a critical mass of us gets connected to our bodies,
we connect to our truth, our inner wisdom, and we don't put
up with the bullshit anymore.

This separation of mind, body, and spirit goes way back.
For the United States context specifically, one needs to look no
further than the attempted genocide of the Indigenous people

whose stolen land we occupy and the enslavement of Black people (with whose bodies the wealth of this country was created). But feeling your feelings, feeling the shock, horror, fear, anger, and sadness brought on by our context, can be subversive in a really powerful way.

One of the most memorable examples I've seen came from an equity expert our company hired years ago. She showed us a picture of white people sitting down to eat a meal and, in the background, you can see a Black person hanging from a tree. This disturbing image is forever seared into my consciousness and her point was well made: there is no way that anyone—*anyone*—could take part in our racist history, regardless of the color of their skin, without dissociating. Whether you are a Black person and afraid this could happen to you next, or a white person knowing in your gut this is absolutely immoral, there is no way you can witness that kind of terrorism without dissociating. And it's still going on today.

The cause of dissociation could have just as easily been the past and present genocide of the Indigenous people on whose stolen land I now live. It could have been the Chinese people who built the railroads under inhumane conditions, the 120,000 Japanese Americans (two-thirds of whom were US born) who were incarcerated en masse during WWII, or the children that were forcibly separated from their families at the US-Mexico border by the Trump administration. It could have been an unarmed Black or Brown person being shot in the back by the police, or a trans person being brutally murdered. It causes trauma. And trauma causes our bodies to separate us from the locus of the trauma in order to survive and to minimize the extent of the fear and pain we feel about what's happening.

These are really intense examples, but they foreground the many ways we dissociate from what we see and shut down our feelings. The things that we humans can do to each other are, on one level, too much to bear. So we dissociate. Of course we do. It could be no other way. Therefore, every act of getting present with your own embodied experience, whether it's noticing that you are feeling sad or scared or even just noticing that your butt itches, is fundamentally an act of liberation. Every time you give your body sensations attention, you are reweaving the connective tissue within your own consciousness. And that is the first step to waking up from our collective dystopia.

Every act of connecting with your own body is in some ways a rebellion against this context of oppression. And you can bet your itchy butt there are still some people who are very vested in you not being aware of your body's sensations or feeling your feelings.

There is no way all this harmful stuff going on in the world could continue if even a fractionally greater percentage of the population was more connected to their bodies and feelings. The jig would be up.

Your body is the nucleus of your personal power. It is the primary building block for creating change in the world. It all starts right inside you.

You might get a lot of pushback for feeling your feelings. People will tell you it's inappropriate or unprofessional, or that it makes them uncomfortable. People will deny your feelings and tell you that you shouldn't feel that way. The question is, Who does it serve to believe that? Who benefits from you being disconnected from your own thoughts and feelings? Not you, not our collective liberation, and not the world. Just a very small group of people who happen to have a lot of power right now.

Many people are scared to feel fully because they think they'll lose control, the feeling will never go away, or they will get sucked down into some dark abyss. But the opposite is true. It is in trying to avoid your feelings that you remain stuck.

When I first started exploring body wisdom in my apprenticeship with Kathlyn Hendricks, I found feeling my feelings really difficult. I remember telling my wife, Christine, that something just didn't feel right to me. She asked me where I felt it and what I was feeling, and I truly went into a fog of confusion, and all I could utter was "I don't know . . . It just feels bad."

That was the best I could do at the time. Now that I've developed an awareness and a wider vocabulary for my own embodied experience, I might tell you, "I was thinking about that person who yelled at me in the parking lot, and I noticed my stomach is still clenched tight. I felt scared then and I still do now." Being able to feel and give voice to my feelings has been extremely liberating for me and made me much more effective as a change leader. Let's explore what might happen for you next.

Allowing Yourself to Feel Your Feelings

When you are able to fully inhabit your own body, you are able to make a conscious decision to access the deeper wisdom your feelings are attempting to communicate with and use that to get back into your essence. When you embrace your feelings and allow them to move through you, there is always a gift on the other side.

So, let's get started. First, realize that feelings come in waves. So if you notice you're having a feeling, all you need to do is keep breathing and focus your attention on the sensations in your body. At first it may seem overwhelming, but as time passes you'll notice that, like a wave crashing ashore, the feeling will come, and then, eventually, it will go, on its own timeline. Your job isn't to get rid of your feelings; it's simply to *feel* them.

Taking the time to notice, acknowledge, and be with whatever you're feeling (without blaming yourself or someone else for that feeling) opens up the possibility of shifting from unconsciously reacting (and keeping the Drama Triangle going) to consciously responding.

Reacting keeps oppressive drama dynamics in place and can even amplify them. Responding transforms whatever is happening into something new and different. Being able to respond carefully is required if you want to make real change in the world.

Much of the time, you can't control the external circumstances around you, but you can control whether and how you choose to respond. Minimizing unconscious reactivity and choosing to respond thoughtfully to any given situation is the essential skill for creating a context for your work that is rooted in solidarity with others and likely to bring forth each person's very best.

Many years ago, I went to an osteopath because my knees hurt. He prescribed orthotics and a session or two with a shaman. Being a Californian, I, of course, did both. The shaman told me that some people are put on this earth to be a filter for trauma. That if you think of intergenerational trauma as a flowing river, some people are on this earth to hop in that river and filter out the trauma as a gift to future generations. I don't know if that is true or not. But filtering out trauma and initiating healing for myself and for as many people as possible is part of what I'm up to in this lifetime. What I know for myself, and what I've seen in others, is that everyone around me benefits when I'm able to get myself into the present moment as often and reliably as possible. When I fully inhabit my being and allow myself to feel the waves of feelings before responding, what emerges from my full presence is always in service of transformation.

It all starts within. This is the inner work of being a change agent. When you allow yourself to fully experience and integrate your emotions, you are serving that filter function my shaman friend was talking about. You're more able to bring clarity and love to your choices and relationships as your outer expression lines up with your inner experience.

All day long, you have opportunities to return to your own inner experience, to listen to your body wisdom, to feel your feelings, and to choose whether or not you're willing in any given moment to be a filter for some of that gunk flowing down that river. Taking time to center yourself in your body is what opens up the door to leveraging your full personal power.

This is how new contexts are able to emerge and flourish—by each of us reclaiming ourselves first. These new contexts are the building blocks for healing yourself and repairing the world. This reclaiming of ourselves is how each of us can influence the world around us, no matter what our relative power is in any given situation. Grounded in embodied truth, expressed through conscious choice, your essence can move mountains.

So it's time to dive into those feelings. Let's double-click on fear first, then we'll explore the gifts of anger, sadness, sexual feelings, and joy.

Your Fear

Remember all those organizational dynamics we faced in part I of the book? They're largely driven by fear.

Indecision? Fear.

Blame and criticism? Fear.

Micromanagement? Fear.

Overwork and overwhelm? Fear.

Whatever else that's messed up in your organization? It's probably being driven by fear.

There's nothing wrong with fear. You're alive today because your ancestors had the good sense to run away from lions and tigers and bears. Fear is necessary for survival, and it has a purpose.

When you are threatened and your fear response is activated, a ton of physiological processes kick into gear and you are primed to freeze, flee, fight, or faint. The only problem is that when you are in fear mode you cannot simultaneously be in the happy-calm state from which lasting and sustainable change is forged. Our brains and bodies simply don't work that way.

We had a saying back in the military, when I used to jump out of perfectly good airplanes and helicopters. We'd look at one another and say, "If you're scared, say you're scared." We were doing dangerous things and we understood that it was actually much safer for everyone involved if we were honest about our fears. My friend Susan Jane reminds me that for herself and other people of color, paying attention to her fear is an important and valid tool for safety.

Whenever I find myself in a messed-up work situation, the first questions I ask myself are "Is anybody else feeling scared right now? What am *I* feeling scared of right now?" That curiosity opens the door to deeper exploration.

Fear tends to hang out around your belly. It might feel like a clenching or butterflies in your stomach. If you're in the early days of exploring your body intelligence, you might just notice something feels off. In response to fear you might freeze, flee, fight, or faint, or do a combination of all four. Becoming familiar with your own patterns will help you notice when you are feeling scared so you can get back into your body and return to your essence.

When someone directs blame or criticism at me, I ask the same question: "I wonder what they're feeling scared about?" Again, that's all that's going on. They're scared. They may not even know it, and they most likely haven't yet learned how to express their fear directly. Then I bring my curiosity inward. Upon hearing this blame, what do I feel scared about? Here are some similar situations and examples of ways I ask myself this question:

- When I notice myself blaming or criticizing any-one or anything, I stop myself and ask, "I wonder what I'm feeling scared about right now?"
- When I'm burning the midnight oil and taking one for the team, I ask myself, "What am I most afraid of?"
- When someone in my group cannot make a deci-sion to save their life, I ask myself, "I wonder what we're all feeling scared about right now?"
- When I am micromanaging someone, I ask myself, "What am I afraid will happen if I let go?"
- And when I have been micromanaged, it was helpful to check in with both myself and the person micromanaging me about how I and they were feeling and if maybe fear had become a member of our team. Am I scared that maybe I'm not actually qualified to do my job? Am I scared that maybe I don't have sufficient judgment to make good decisions on my own?

Sometimes your fears will make sense to you, and some-times they will seem entirely mysterious. But they show up at work anyway. We like to think of our lives as compartmen-talized into nice, neat little boxes labeled "work" and "home." Maybe you're going through a divorce, and this is the *One. Thing. In. Your. Life. You. Can. Control.* Maybe your mom never told you she was proud. The reason why you're scared could be anything; the source of your fear doesn't really matter. The most important question is, How can you get yourself out of your reptile brain and back into your more creative prefrontal cortex?

Use Your Own Oxygen Mask First

Your ability to stay curious, especially in the face of fear, is a way of using your personal power to repair the world without breaking yourself. As a general rule, I want to caution you against telling other people that they are scared. It is one thing to ask, "Hmm, I wonder if it's possible that we're all feeling scared right now?" It's another thing entirely to tell someone else how they're feeling. Don't do that. It never goes well.

The best advice I can give you is to start with yourself. Get really good at noticing when you feel scared and get really good at moving through that back to your grounded essence. Then you can venture out into playing with others. Shifting yourself from fear to presence is a huge way to use your three feet of influence.

But *how* can you do that? What do you do when you're feeling scared? Here's an exercise I use for myself and with people I'm coaching. I've found it works wonders when we're feeling scared.

Act Now: Moving Through Fear with Blurt/ Breathe/Move and Journal

Before you start on this exercise, I want to caution that you should do this at a time and in a place where you feel safe to explore. And if you do this with others, make sure they are people with whom you feel emotional safety.

This will only take six minutes. Take a few deep breaths, then proceed:

1. **Blurt.** Set a timer for two minutes and have at it: get to the kernel of what's nagging at your soul in a situation you've identified. Be as unenlightened and as unprofessional and unpackaged as you possibly can. Say things that are utterly inappropriate to say. In this "what happened" step, allow yourself to keep going longer if you need to. That said, I've never seen anyone need more than two minutes to blurt out the nugget of truth they didn't quite know how to express properly. It's not about being proper here; it's about being honest with yourself.

2. **Breathe.** Set a timer for two minutes and bring your attention to your breath. Feel your inbreath. Notice your outbreath. Nothing more. Nothing less. If you get distracted, just bring your attention back to your inbreath and outbreath. This is the core of many meditation practices.

   (Sometimes when I'm doing executive coaching and I notice a client is starting to spiral, I'll suggest we just stop and breathe for a minute. They always agree enthusiastically, and we breathe together in silence. And they're *always* energetically in a different place as a result of doing so. More grounded. More present. You've got to be present to win. Breathing is one way to reliably get there, and it only takes a minute or two.)

3. **Move.** Set a timer for two minutes and go for a little walk. Get your body moving. If you want to play your favorite song and make it a dancing walk, all the better. Anything you need to do to get your

body moving. This will help the fear chemicals in your body move through you.

Another thing you might try while you're moving is called Fear Melters. Dr. Kathlyn Hendricks developed these as movement antidotes to the four primary fear signatures: freeze, flee, fight, and faint.[5]

4. **Journal.** Jot down each aha that emerged as a result of this process. Anything that's true for you will do. Often in the course of doing this, it will become blatantly obvious what you are feeling, whether that's being angry, sad, scared, or any combination of the three. That's a great discovery. Sometimes what will surface is something that you want: a request. All the better. What you're after is something that is authentically true for you and something that is unarguable, including your feelings.

Complete this sentence: What I really want is . . . _____

_____

_____

_____

_____

_____

Anger, Sadness, Joy, and Sexual Feelings

I'm a big fan of bringing your body to work with you. Your body will know something isn't right before your rational brain will. And that's useful information. While fear is a significant

---

5. You can find instructions for how to do Fear Melters at https://foundationforconsciousliving.org/big_leap_home/unlocking-the-fear-code-and-accessing-essence-power/.

driver of oppression and an obstacle to solving some of our biggest problems, we would be remiss not to give a quick nod to some of the other primary emotions that might be present.

Anger

Anger manifests itself in a clenched jaw, a tension headache, stiff shoulders, or a sore back—all the way down to your sacrum for deep-seated resentments. It is the appropriate and natural response to injustice. It is useful when used to restore boundaries to their proper place. A lot of people I coach are afraid to feel or express their anger and, as we covered earlier, the risks associated with expressing anger are not evenly distributed within our society.

One of our fellows, Lindsay Hill, founder of Sojourner Advising, shared her learnings and growth around anger with me, and I share it here because I think it's really important for change leaders to understand this. Lindsay said:

> As a Black woman in the US (where we typically only accept anger from white men), it is hard to lean into anger and even more scary to express it in spaces that are centered around white supremacy culture. There are times when I've been worried, annoyed, or just had an itch (literally) that I couldn't scratch and have been read as angry by colleagues thanks to centuries of stereotypes and dehumanizing portrayals of Black women in the media. While I used to ignore my own anger, as a way to combat these stereotypes, I've now learned to appreciate anger as an opportunity for reflection. I try to take the time to listen for what my anger is really

trying to show me. Is it fear? Sadness? Pain?
There is always a deeper emotion underneath.
Now, even in the most extreme moments, I'm
getting better at interpreting rage as a signal I
must listen to. I have a right to be angry and
turning to courage is a powerful way to hold
space for anger while engaging in work that will
actually transform the systems, structures, and
relationships of which I'm a part.

She goes on to share that sometimes she has felt pressure
by white people to get rid of her anger. The world she wants
to create is one in which white people are more invested in
changing the circumstances that give rise to the anger in the
first place than they are in policing the emotions of Black people. Amen to that.

There is an extra layer of mental gymnastics that Lindsay
as a Black woman has to perform to calculate when and how
to express her anger if she wants to have the desired outcome
of making things more just and fairer. Not only does she have
to do an additional risk assessment that someone else may not
need to do, but she has to tend to her own self-care. Sometimes
this means screaming in her car after a meeting. Sometimes it
means celebrating with her loved ones. What we can learn from
her story is that anger is an important cue for all of us. On the
other side of feeling our anger is the invitation to use courage to
change the circumstances that caused it in the first place.

The bottom line is that anger is a natural result of being
thwarted and an appropriate emotion when an injustice has
occurred or a boundary has been crossed. It shows up when
you're getting something you don't want or not getting something you do want. Whenever possible, use the energy of your
anger to right the wrong or restore the boundary. Listen to
your anger!

Sadness

Sadness is generally felt in the chest and throat area and is often accompanied by tears. It is a function of experiencing a real or imagined loss of some kind. Sadness is your body's way of telling you there is something to let go of. Personally, I go to great lengths to avoid feeling sadness, although I am learning to befriend it. When I don't allow my sad feelings to move through, they just stick around. Sadness wants to be expressed.

One of the best examples of befriending sadness I've witnessed in my life came during an acupuncture session in NYC. I was in my session with Marion Skelly (who has since passed on) when her old-fashioned, literally hanging-on-the-wall corded phone rang. She answered and I overheard her side of the conversation. It was clear something bad had happened and Marion started to cry. I asked what the matter was and through tears she said, "I just found out a friend of mine died, and I'm going to miss him." And she sat still for a moment, her face expressing a sadness that couldn't find words. I sat quietly, not knowing what to do or say. After a few moments Marion said, "And I don't want to die, either." Then she took a deep breath, her sadness lifted, and she returned to treating me. All this took place in a span of maybe one minute.

Now you could think maybe she was Hero-ing me and didn't want to allow herself to feel her feelings. But I don't think that was what was going on. I think Marion was so practiced in being with emotions that she had cultivated an advanced ability to be with what she was feeling and allow it to move through rather than get stuck. Out of the many, many things I learned from my acupuncture sessions with her, this one was perhaps the most profound: feel your sadness move through you.

I've noticed that often when someone starts to cry or expresses sadness, people lurch for Kleenex and want them to feel better. What if instead we invited people to feel their sadness all the way through to the gift on the other side?

Bottom line: Sadness is a natural emotion when we're experiencing a loss. And losses happen. It's OK to let those tears flow.

Joy

Joy is different for different people, but for me it is more of a full-body, champagne-bubble kind of experience. Almost like an effervescence of upward energy. Joy is a big message that the context I am in works for me, and that I can fully be myself. When I experience joy, my sense of it is "Yes, please, more of this!"

Joy is a powerful body signal indicating whom I want to spend more time with, what I want to spend more time doing, and where I want to be.

Joy is also a powerful force for attracting people to your work to change the world. It is just as powerful an emotion as fear, sadness, and anger. As you notice the contexts that generate joy for yourself and your colleagues, get curious about what is creating that feeling and ask, How can we do more of that?

Sexual Feelings

I almost left sexual feelings out of this book, but that would have been a huge mistake. How do your sexual feelings relate to leading social change? I have two thoughts about it that I hope you will consider in your own practice as a change leader.

First, it is in the denial of even talking about our sexual feelings that we create all kinds of additional problems. In the army, we used to call it a "zipper incident" when somebody somewhere would have sex with somebody when they weren't supposed to, whether it was because it was an affair or with someone in the chain of command. Want to guarantee that you will have a zipper incident in your organization? Make it totally taboo to talk about sexual feelings. For example, consider the tremendous harm that has been perpetrated by some priests in the Catholic Church, an organization that is notorious for its suppression of sexual feelings. I rest my case.

Second, one of the best things about being a human is getting to feel and enjoy your sexual feelings. It's your birthright, and for me to deny that or render that invisible by omission would be to miss out on the intelligence and information our bodies are trying to communicate to us, just like any other feeling. The Conscious Leadership Forum created a wonderful map that details low, medium, and high levels of feelings. In the category of sexual feelings, as one might expect, we find words like "aroused," "passionate," and "sensual," but there are also words like "inspired," "stimulated," "excited," and "euphoric." When I first encountered this topography of feelings, my thought was *Who knew that I am having sexual feelings all the time!* And the truth is, I am. In fact, my sexual feelings are the most reliable indicator to me of my own aliveness and authentic enthusiasm for any given possibility.

So there you have it: sexual feelings.

One pearl of wisdom I learned from Kathlyn Hendricks that feels appropriate to pass along here is something I've heard her say many times: Go ahead and enjoy the heck out of all your sexual feelings; just be very smart about expressing them. That's basically it. No big deal.

If you want to delve into this further, I recommend adrienne maree brown's *Pleasure Activism* where she shares her philosophy of transforming individuals and the entire world through—you guessed it—sexual feelings.

When you allow yourself to feel your feelings, there is always a gift for you on the other side. For Lindsay, her anger was a cue that something was unjust and there was an opportunity, should she consciously choose it, for her to be courageous. For Marion, her sadness was a reminder of how much she loved her friend and how much she appreciated being alive. For all of us, our joy is an invitation to pay attention to what is working and do more of that!

Act Now: Feelings Inventory

This exercise is one of my very favorites for feeling my feelings and getting through to the gift of clarity on the other side. Related to the challenges you want to address, what feelings are you now aware that you have? Go ahead and list them all. You might be all over the map and that's OK. _____

_____

_____

_____

_____

_____

Do they tend to fit into a certain category (sad, angry, scared, joyful, sexual) or are they all over the map? _____

_____

_____

_____

_____

Are there any feelings you tend to avoid allowing yourself to feel? _____

_____

_____

_____

_____

Are you willing to allow yourself to welcome all your feelings as wisdom here to help you? _____

_____

Act Now: Clearing the Pipes

This is another one of my favorite exercises and, between you and me, I always keep a couple of printouts of this handout nearby just in case I can't quite put my finger on what's bothering me. Nancy Stubbs shared this exercise with me, and she learned it from Kathlyn Hendricks at the Hendricks Institute.

First, set a timer for one minute and simply breathe and notice any body sensations that might arise. Pay careful attention to your stomach, chest, throat, neck, shoulders, and back. Tightness and pain in any of those areas can be your body's way of trying to get your attention. Then just write whatever comes to mind for you. Stay with the first five questions until you feel a sense of completeness with all of them. Only then move to the last question.

1. I feel scared that . . . _____
   _____
   _____
   _____

2. I feel sad that . . . _____
   _____
   _____
   _____

3. I feel angry that . . . _____
   _____
   _____

_____

_____

4. I feel joyful that . . . _____

_____

_____

_____

_____

5. I feel sexual that . . . _____

_____

_____

_____

_____

6. What I really want is . . . _____

_____

_____

_____

_____

The reason feeling our feelings is such an important skill for change leaders is that it both keeps us healthy and whole and gives us the gift of clarity on the other side.

Be Honest About What You Want

You'll notice that all the Act Now exercises in this chapter ended with the same question: What do you really want?

Reliably being able to know what you really want is . . . everything. And the answer is *always in your body*. Not that your head isn't part of your body (it is), but it's not the only place you "know" things.

Sometimes it's not easy to discern what you really want because you're still caught in the grip of fear. Fear will prevent you from having access to your full creativity. Instead, you will distract yourself on the Drama Triangle, alternating between your Hero, Villain, and Victim personas. So if you are still feeling the grip of fear, please repeat the Blurt/Breathe/Move and Journal exercise or the Clearing the Pipes exercise as many times as you need to before coming back to this page.

When you're not in a place of fear, you have access to your deepest essence. In working with thousands of change leaders, I've yet to find someone's essence to have nefarious intentions. What your essence wants (whatever that may be) can most likely be of service to the weaving together of the web of life. In some ways, repairing the world isn't so much about doing things "out there" as it is about clearing out the gunk "in here." You can trust your essence.

Before we move on to the next chapter, let's take one more moment to do an exercise to really capture your innermost truth.

Act Now: What Do You Really Want? Tuning in to Your Full-Body Knowing

Do this in a private space where you will not be interrupted.

Set a timer for three minutes and write down your answer to the question below. See what emerges for you. Leave it open ended—it can be about work or your personal life. Jot down everything that comes across your consciousness. Have fun with it.

What do I really want? _____

_____

_____

_____

_____

_____

_____

_____

_____

_____

_____

Now, go back one by one to each of the items you wrote down.

Say each item you identified above out loud then close your eyes. Notice how you feel in your body as you say what you want out loud. When I do this, for example, sometimes I notice my balance shifting forward or backward. Sometimes I notice a downward push of energy in my chest. Sometimes I notice butterflies of excitement in my stomach. And sometimes I notice little fireworks of joy in my chest. Your body will give you different cues because each of us is unique.

The purpose of this exercise is to practice opening up to what it is you really want and to begin to use your body wisdom in support of accessing your deeper wisdom.

After you've listened to your body's response to each of the items you've identified in the initial brainstorm, go back and circle the item(s) where you noticed the most aliveness in your body.

This is where the good stuff is for you. This is incredibly useful information, and you can refer back to it like a road map in the future, too. Imagine what might happen if you allow yourself to really go for it?

Chapter 6 Takeaways

- When you don't allow yourself to feel your feelings or others to feel theirs, you are reproducing oppression. It may be conscious or unconscious, but the impact is the same.

- When you create the space for yourself to feel your feelings and others to feel theirs, you avail yourself of the gift on the other side: clarity.
- Fear is a natural response to a threat and is simply chemicals moving through your body. When you're in a fear state, you lose access to your creativity as all your body's resources are going toward ensuring your survival.
- Sadness is a natural response to loss.
- Anger is a natural response to being thwarted and to injustice. It lets you know a boundary has been crossed and wants to be restored.
- Sexual feelings are tied up with your creativity and aliveness. It's all connected, and, in the workplace, it is helpful to differentiate between feeling your feelings and expressing them.
- Joyful feelings let you know you are headed in the right direction.
- Your emotions are generating massive insights to help you clarify your commitment, if only you will listen to them.
- Leadership is a full-body sport. Bring your body to work with you!

CHAPTER 7

THE POWER OF COMMITMENT

Just as you can know what a system is designed to do by paying attention to its outcomes, you can also discover what you personally are committed to by looking at the results you're getting. Both systems and individuals can operate unconsciously or consciously. If you don't like the results you are getting in some aspect of your life or your efforts to change the world, now is the time to bring your unconscious commitments up to the surface for examination. In the full light of day, you can consider whether or not your commitments are helping you create the change you want to make or sabotaging your every move.

If you're not aligned, deep down in your heart, you secretly have one foot out the door. In other words, you are in limbo.

If you have any ambivalence whatsoever about what you want, you're stuck in the middle. Nothing really changes, and you can find yourself untethered and ineffective.

When you are in limbo, your unconscious commitments run the show. You say you *want* X, but you have an *unconscious commitment* to Y. Guess which wins every time? That's right. Y wins. Every. Single. Time.

This is what being in limbo means. You cannot repair the world when you are in limbo. In fact, being in limbo does far more harm than good. And if you keep this pattern going, you will become resentful. It may appear as though you are resenting someone or something outside yourself, but underneath that you are usually only resentful of yourself for not choosing something different, for not having the courage to leave or at least exploring other options even if it doesn't entail leaving. This resentment is toxic.

When I was a young captain in the military, I was invited to return to West Point as a professor. Included in the deal was fully funded graduate school at the best school I could get into. It was a tempting offer, but I was still living in the closet and had major reservations about continuing to hide my sexual orientation.

One of my dearest mentors was also a professor there, and I felt comfortable confiding my dilemma to him. Even though he could have used my disclosure against me, I knew I could trust him. He spoke with his colleagues and offered me assurances that my sexual orientation would not be a problem and that they had my back. But I still couldn't decide. I was in limbo, unable to commit.

Later that summer, we both happened to be in Washington, DC, so we met at a restaurant on Connecticut Avenue and discussed my fate. I didn't know what I wanted, and I was ambivalent about this opportunity. Part of me wanted to go to graduate school and teach at West Point. I had always wanted to be a teacher when I was a kid. But part of me knew that not being completely honest about my identity was wearing away at my soul, and that part of me was saying I should get out of the military entirely and go be an instructor at the National Outdoor Leadership School (now just known as NOLS), helping young people develop leadership skills through outdoor adventures. I couldn't choose. This is what limbo looks like.

Finally, my friend said, "Becky, you have to decide. Let's flip a coin. Heads, you go out into the civilian world and start a new life. Tails, you come back to West Point and teach with me." This sounded like a perfectly good idea to me at the time, so I agreed.

He flipped the coin. Heads it was! He slumped down onto the bar and I felt a little bit of disbelief, sadness, and disappointment that I had made a major life decision based on chance. I almost said, "Let's go for two out of three," but I stopped myself from saying that out loud.

Who knows what I'd be doing now if I had followed that impulse? And there was something about how dramatically my mentor seemed to respond to the outcome of the coin toss that I, too, started to believe it was real. That I had actually decided. So I went back to work the next day and submitted my resignation from the army. Over a coin toss. None of this would have happened had I known about the power of commitment.

Commitment is being clear on and anchored by what you really want. Once you are clear on what you are committed to, each new decision in front of you (and there will be thousands) is simply a matter of tuning into your yeses and nos and seeing what happens. If you don't like the results, most of the time you can change your mind and do something different. You're never too young to get clear on what you are willing to commit to. And you're never too old to get out of limbo!

In this chapter, we're going to unpack the concept of commitment and dig into some best practices for getting clear on what you want and how you can step confidently out of limbo and into what you really want.

Knowing Your Yeses and Nos

Knowing and expressing your yeses and your nos is an essential skill for getting out of limbo. You're not going to use your yeses and nos to screw people over or become incredibly selfish. You're going to use this skill to get into alignment so that we can bring your whole and best self to the work. Giving yourself permission to know your no is countercultural in a lot of the professions that require people to give and give and give, but bear with me. This could change your life.

What I mean by "your yeses" is the people, places, things, and experiences in your life that you feel an authentic, resonant, full-body yes to. By "your nos" I similarly mean the people, places, things, and experiences in your life that cause you to detect a no anywhere in your body.

Notice I didn't say "calculate in your mind" a yes or a no. This isn't about a lengthy analysis or pros and cons. Nor is this about exploring what you "should" do. You listen to your body for signature cues indicating whether or not you want something in your life. Let's start with your yeses.

Knowing Your Yeses

I've found that acting from my full-body yes is incredibly useful in navigating the work of social change. If I haven't quite gotten to a full-body yes (the alignment of my head, my heart, and my body), I know whatever it is that I'm contemplating is not quite the best answer yet. So I stay with it a little longer before I take action. Once I take action from a fully aligned place, there's a much greater likelihood that I will have the effect I desire.

Let's start with exploring what you have a full-body yes to. Please do the following exercise before moving on to the next section.

Act Now: Know Your Yeses

Set a timer for three minutes and jot down everything you want that comes to your mind. Don't filter it and don't worry about your yeses and your nos yet. This is just brainstorming to get your creative ideas flowing.

What I really want is . . . _____

_____

_____

_____

_____

_____

_____

_____

_____

_____

At the end of the three minutes, stand if you are able to, as that can be helpful in detecting some of the microhints your body is going to give you next. If you're not able to stand, this can be done seated as well.

Next, state each separate item that you want out loud, one at a time, and notice any signals your body sends you. As you say each want out loud, one at a time, tune in to your body signals and notice what you feel. Where in your body did you feel what you felt? What was happening to the energy in your body? Which words or colors or sounds came to mind for you with each one? See if you're able to discern any trends in terms of how your body tells you that you have a yes.

For example, when I have a full-body yes, I notice an opening in my heart and chest area. My energy seems to be moving upward when I have a yes. But those are my unique body-wisdom cues. This will be a chance for you to begin to notice yours.

What were your three biggest yeses, the things that you really want? _____

_____

_____

_____

Where in your body did you notice the clearest yes energy? Write your body signals for a yes down here for future reference. _____

_____

_____

_____

_____

Let's suppose that you now have access to your full-body yes and are willing to listen to your deepest wisdom. Remember how this feels. This feeling of what a full-body yes feels like will be something you will want to return to again and again, as you're making decisions and navigating the uncertainty and complexity of leading social change.

Sometimes you might experience a full-body yes and, in addition to that, you might notice a layer of fear on top of it. That's totally normal. You might feel confused and worry that maybe that means it's a no. Doing this exercise several times will help you gain a real understanding of your own body and when it is saying yes, when it is saying no, and when it is saying,

"I feel scared." It takes some practice to be able to discern the difference, but it's well worth the effort.

If you feel yes plus some fear, go back and do the Blurt/Breathe/Move and Journal exercise and then try again. Keep going until something emerges on the other side of your fear.

You might be wondering, *What if my "yes" was really a "meh"?*

So, here's the next pearl of wisdom that I want to share with you: *Anything other than a full-body yes is a no.* Period. Allow that to sink in for a minute.

I know what you're thinking: "But, Becky, I have so many nos." Yup. I know. So, let's explore your nos, too.

Knowing Your Nos

As important as knowing your yeses is knowing your nos. A reminder: by "your nos" I mean the people, places, things, and experiences in your life that cause you to feel a decrease in aliveness. Our bodies are trying to help us! Just as I believe that honoring your yeses is a service to the unfolding of the universe, so, too, I believe that honoring your nos is necessary.

For decades I believed the only way I could really make a difference and also get ahead in my career was to say yes to things I didn't actually want to do. I was literally taught, "This is what you need to do to get ahead." So I get it. I've been there and done that myself. I understand how hard it is to differentiate between what's aligned with my own essence and what other people expect of me. But overriding your no is one of the fastest roads to forfeiting your personal power.

When you override your nos—when you notice that you have a no but ignore it and say yes instead—you put yourself in limbo. And I've seen all kinds of justifications for overriding a no. Here are a few favorites:

- "My team needs me."
- "This sucks, but it will help me get ahead."
- "I'm probably the only person who could do this the way it needs to be done."
- "If I say no, they'll think I'm selfish."
- "I don't want to fulfill a stereotype."
- "I need to do this to survive."

There are also significant external pressures to say yes rooted in our white dominant culture:

- The scarcity mentality that demands we "do more with less"
- Deadlines that perpetuate a never-ending sense of urgency
- The perfectionism that generates a lot of busy-work and wasted energy

The list goes on. There are also differences across identities regarding who gets to say yes and, most important, who gets to say no. For some of us, saying no is a privilege we take for granted. For others, saying no can tee up fears for our own survival. All these differences across societal and positional power are real. And yet . . .

Regardless of where you are situated relative to these other realms of power, you *always* have your personal power. Nobody can take away your ability to make choices or take action for yourself. Your no is yours and yours alone. Nobody can take away your no.

The problem is, somehow over the course of your life, you may have internalized the message that you don't really get to have a say in things. This might trace back to the way your parents raised you or what you learned in school. It doesn't really matter where you picked it up, if deep down you believe that what you want doesn't matter. Eventually, you are going to lose the ability to even discern what you really want in the first place. Internalizing this oppressive construct not only reduces your effectiveness at work but also reduces your joy, satisfaction, and even your health.

So here's an alternative to try on for size: never agree to anything on the spot when you're aware of any inner hesitation. Give yourself twenty-four hours to tune in to your yeses and your nos away from the energetic force field of others.

For starters, though, let's explore your nos the same way we explored your yeses.

Act Now: Know Your Nos

Set a timer for three minutes and jot down everything you don't want that comes to your mind. This is just brainstorming to get your creative ideas flowing.

I have a no to . . . _____

_____

_____

_____

_____

_____

_____

_____

At the end of the three minutes, stand if you are able to, as that can be helpful in detecting some of the microhints your body is going to give you next. If you're not able to stand, this can be done seated as well.

When I have a no to something, I notice a sinking downward energy that starts in my chest. This will be a chance for you to begin to notice your unique no cues.

Next, state each separate item that you have a no to out loud, one at a time, and notice any signals your body sends you. As you say each no, tune in to your body signals and notice what you feel. Where in your body did you feel what you felt? What was happening to the energy in your body? Which words or colors or sounds come to mind for you with each one? See if you're able to discern any trends in terms of how your body tells you that you have a no.

Write your top three nos down here: _____

_____

_____

_____

Where in your body did you notice the clearest no energy? Write your body signals for a no down here for future reference. _____

_____

_____

_____

I want to encourage you to keep a "no notebook" for at least a week. A month would be even better. Keep it with you at all times and jot down anything you notice you have a hesitation or a no to. You don't have to do anything about it yet. All you have to do for now is notice when your body is telling you no.

Your Permission to Honor Your Yeses and Nos

If I could, I would give everybody on the planet a great big permission slip to honor their nos. Whenever I include the Know Your Nos exercise in our workshops, I see so much relief and liberation on people's faces as they open up to the truth of their no. It's like they're saying, "Wait a minute, I get to say no?"

Yes! Not only do you get to say no, you *must* say no if you want to be effective as a change leader and you also want to stay healthy and sane.

And here's another bonus. You don't even owe anybody an excuse or justification for your no. You just get to have a no. Period.

Do you have any colleagues who always say yes? Have you ever asked them to do something and wondered if they really *want* to do it, if their heart is in it? Do you trust those people? Be honest. There's something a little untrustworthy about someone who always says yes to everything.

I don't know about you, but I'm never sure if they are being truly genuine with me. And I thrive in relationships that are caring *and* authentic. Those two things are not mutually exclusive; they are entwined. It's important to remember that differentials in societal and positional power might make you feel less safe in expressing your nos, because there may be different consequences (see chapter 5 for a refresher on that). At the very least, I want you to know your nos. Even if you're not quite ready to express them yet.

So please give yourself a great big permission slip to honor your nos. We'll cover how to express that in a way that preserves the relationship (assuming you want to) in chapters 9 and 10, where we cover revealing and healthy agreements.

The gift of knowing your no isn't just for you. This is a gift for everyone you know, and we hope you will share it. I especially want to invite you to pay this forward to your colleagues.

Especially if you have positional power. When I make a request, I like to follow by saying, "And please know, that your no is as good as your yes to me." It might seem scary, but giving other people permission to honor their nos will liberate you, too.

I _____ [your name] give myself
permission to know and express my no.

Signed, _____

Act Now: Yeses and Nos Together

Let's circle back for a minute and make sure we have something that's meaningful and important for you to wrestle with before we move forward. Go back to the exercises called Act Now: Know Your Yeses and Act Now: Know Your Nos, and jot down your three biggest yeses and three biggest nos in the space below.

Three Biggest Yeses and Three Biggest Nos

1. _____
2. _____
3. _____

1. _____
2. _____
3. _____

What might your life be like if you honored the inner wisdom of these three yeses and three nos? _____

_____

_____

_____

What would you be doing differently with your time and creativity? _____

_____

_____

_____

_____

Who would you be in community with? _____

_____

_____

_____

What changes would ripple out into the world? _____

_____

_____

_____

Communicating Your Yeses and Nos

Getting clear on what you really want (and what you don't want) is a tremendous accomplishment, so pat yourself on the back or do a little happy dance or whatever you like to do to appreciate yourself. (If you don't have a way to appreciate yourself, we'll be exploring that further in chapter 8.) Once you know your yeses and your nos and how to reliably assess them in the future, you are in a position to communicate them clearly to any other relevant parties.

I remember when I first relearned that I could say no (it took me a few tries!). I was forty-three and had just completed a weekend workshop with Kathlyn Hendricks in California. We had done an experiential exercise to get clear on our yeses and our nos. And I was pumped up to put this new concept to work.

The next morning I had a call with my teammates from the 100,000 Homes Campaign. Someone mentioned that I had been asked to give a keynote at a conference in Tulsa, Oklahoma. I had been traveling almost nonstop, and to my delight and terror, I realized that I felt a no to giving that keynote. Now this is something I was *expected* to do. I gave keynotes all the time as the director of the 100,000 Homes Campaign. It was literally part of my job description. Would I disappoint them? Would they think I wasn't really committed? Would they judge me as being lazy? I mean, I *should* go. Right?

So here's what I managed to eke out on the phone call: "Hey, y'all. I was just at a workshop where I learned to discern between my yeses and my nos, and I realize that I don't actually want to go to Tulsa to give that keynote."

Long pause. I'm imagining my team on the other end of the line in stunned silence.

Then I heard my colleague Linda say this: "I'll go to Tulsa! I'd love to give that keynote!" And she wasn't taking one for the team. She actually *wanted* to go. Turns out Linda loved traveling and she was a natural and gifted public speaker. Linda loved traveling so much that she agreed to speak in North Dakota in December. We wouldn't have tapped into this area of genius for Linda had I not taken the risk of being honest about my own no. It's not that I don't love giving keynotes, by the way. I do! I just needed a time-out from the frequent-flier lifestyle for a little bit back then.

If you have a pattern of saying yes to things you really don't want to do, of sacrificing your personal or family life for your work, of endlessly taking one for the team, or feeling like you have no choice, that is a recipe for resentment and burnout. Remember, it is the Hero persona that cannot say no. Or the inner Villain that says, "You should." Or the Victim persona that says, "I have to." If this is coming up for you, go ahead and interview that persona using the prompts in appendix B.

Your solitary no might not make all the change you want it to make. And it might carry huge risks for you. Or it might be contagious in the best possible way. If you cannot say no, how can anybody trust that you really mean it when you say yes? How can anybody trust you if you're not being honest, starting with yourself?

Knowing and expressing your yeses and nos are essential skills for being able to repair the world without breaking yourself. May you use them in good health—and communicate them with confidence.

Go from Wanting to Willing to Commitment

Refining your wants by honoring your yeses and nos can bring into sharper relief any areas where you may have some ambivalence. Sometimes the solution is straightforward, and you can simply integrate your yeses and nos into what it is you really want, refining as you go. Sometimes by interrogating your yeses and your nos, you discover that what you actually want is something else entirely.

While it's absolutely essential that you know what you want, your wants alone are insufficient for changing a single thing in the outside world. In fact, they are utterly powerless unless they are converted into willingness, and then into the rocket fuel that is a bona fide commitment.

I learned this framework for shifting from wanting to willing to commitment from Kathlyn Hendricks and loved it so much that I wanted to include it here so you can apply it, too.

We'll go through an example first, then create space for you to do this at the end of the chapter.

Be forewarned, though. Commitments are the real deal. They literally set in motion the creation of reality. And I believe that's what we do when we repair the world: create a different reality. I'll just say to be careful what you commit to. Because in my experience I've found that most things I've committed to have one way or another come to fruition. Onward!

Move from Wanting to Willing

So, what do you really want? Here are some wants that I've heard social change leaders express over the years:

- I want Elise to stop criticizing me.
- I want Brenda to stop giving me work over the weekends.
- I want Andre to make a decision.
- I want Molly to be self-sufficient, so I don't have to micromanage her anymore.
- I want Chris to stop micromanaging me.
- I want Brad to stop his offensive behavior toward people with my identity.
- I want to house 100,000 people.

This is where people start. The problem seems like it's outside you, so you want the other person to change. But here's the thing: you can't actually control what other people do or say, so wanting them to change is crazy making.

My challenge to you is to flip the script and make your wants about something that is in your own sphere of influence. Something you can control. And *you* control what you do and say. So the shift would look something like this:

Something you can't control	Something you can control
I want Elise to stop criticizing me.	I want to stop criticizing myself; I want to let Elise's criticism of me roll off my back like water off a duck; I want to work in an organization that is fueled by appreciation.
I want Brenda to stop giving me work over the weekends.	I want to prioritize and receive rest and relaxation each weekend.
I want Andre to make a decision.	I want to be more decisive myself; I want to work on a team where decisions get made.
I want Molly to be self-sufficient, so I don't have to micromanage her anymore.	I want to stop micromanaging Molly.
I want Chris to stop micromanaging me.	I want to stop questioning my own judgment; I want to be unfazed by Chris's questioning of me; I want to work on a team where my experience is valued.
I want Brad to stop his offensive behavior toward people with my identity.	I want to work for someone who is committed to justice. I want to work for someone who is respectful of others.
I want to house 100,000 people.	I want to lead a team that creates the conditions that result in 100,000 people being housed.

If you think about it, the word "want" literally means "lack" or "don't currently have." So whenever you say the phrase "I want _____," you're doing nothing more than stating what is already true. It's a start, but not the stuff of planetary transformation.

Once you're clear on what you want and it is something that is within your own sphere of control, the next step is to

THE POWER OF COMMITMENT

check with yourself and see if you are able to shift from wanting something to actually being willing to have it happen.

Look at what happens when we substitute *willing* for *want*:

I want . . .	I am willing . . .
I want to stop criticizing myself; I want to let Elise's criticism of me roll off my back like water off a duck; I want to work in an organization that is fueled by appreciation.	I am willing to stop criticizing myself; I am willing to let Elise's criticism roll off my back like water off a duck; I am willing to work in an organization that is fueled by appreciation.
I want to prioritize and receive rest and relaxation each weekend.	I am willing to prioritize and receive rest and relaxation each weekend.
I want to be more decisive myself; I want to work on a team where decisions get made.	I am willing to be more decisive myself; I am willing to work on a team where decisions get made.
I want to stop micromanaging Molly.	I am willing to stop micromanaging Molly.
I want to stop questioning my own judgment; I want to be unfazed by Chris's questioning of me; I want to work on a team where my experience is valued.	I am willing to stop questioning my own judgment; I am willing to be unfazed by Chris's questioning of me; I am willing to work on a team where my experience is valued.
I want to work for someone who is committed to justice. I want to work for someone who is respectful of others.	I am willing to request a different supervisor; I am willing to report Brad to HR; I am willing to look for a different job at a different company; I am willing to organize with my colleagues to create a more just workplace.
I want to lead a team that creates the conditions that result in 100,000 people being housed in the US.	I am willing to do everything in my power to create the conditions that result in 100,000 people being housed in the US.

Notice the difference there? The shift is from stating what is true (always a good start) to expressing what you are willing to do about it. This puts you in the driver's seat of your own life and linguistically shifts you from being at the effect of people and forces around you to being an agent of change in your own life. This is progress! This is alignment in action. Willing is a great place to be, but the next step is the most important.

When you're ready to take it up a notch, you can try on committing for size. Committing isn't something that you want to force yourself into before you're ready. Don't muscle yourself to a place of being ready to make a commitment. Allow yourself to marinate in willingness for an hour or two, a day or two, or as long as it takes until your choice becomes much clearer to you. Make sure it is what you really want and what you are really willing to do.

The way I know that I am ready to move from being willing to committing is I feel a sense of something dropping deeper into my core and I hear a voice in my head saying, "Oh, I'm not just willing. I am able to commit now." It's almost like shifting up with a manual gearshift in a car, but it's in my body. It's hard to explain precisely. It's a sense that I'm fully available to take it to the next level.

Move from Willing to Committing

When you're ready, it is time to step into a commitment of your choosing. I think of commitment as a sacred pact between myself and the universe. You might see it as something between yourself and your higher self, your higher power, your god, your goddess, etc. Note that commitment does not require any other human beings. This is not "I'll do it if you do it." That's an agreement, and we'll cover that more in chapter 10.

When I commit to something, it sets in motion my unconscious brain in a way that wanting and willing just can't do. That doesn't mean it automatically happens. Quite the contrary. What usually happens after I commit to something is the universe sends me a pop quiz to see if I really mean it. That's to be expected, and the thing to do in that moment is to catch it happening and recommit. Do not get sucked back into the vortex of your prior unconscious commitment.

Here is a quick example: While I was writing this book, the COVID-19 pandemic hit. Up until the pandemic, 100 percent of my business's revenue came from in-person events and workshops. So you can imagine some fear came up for me as we figured out how we would pivot. I used many of the same techniques I've shared in this book: facing into my challenges, facing into how I was on the Drama Triangle, allowing myself to feel my feelings, and tuning into my yeses and my nos.

After going through those steps, I had just clarified my commitment and it went like this: *I commit to channeling my creative energy to support progressive social change leaders in making their big dent in the universe.*

Literally, the next day after I had clarified my commitment, I received an email from an agency that helps small businesses get government contracts. "Would you be interested in helping the US *Navy* with leadership development?" they asked.

Being a West Point grad, my first response was *Navy? Hell no!* But my second thought was to basically see dollar signs. A government contract could help our business survive the pandemic. I was doing a happy dance and about a minute into it I realized, *Oh! That's a pop quiz from the universe!* It wants to know if I'm serious about helping *social change leaders* make their big dent. And I was. So I politely declined. This is where knowing your nos comes in handy, by the way. And I felt this whoosh of energy and doubled down on my commitment and aligned with my bigger yes.

Let's see what happens when we substitute "commit" for "willing" using the same examples from before:

I am willing . . .	I commit . . .
I am willing to stop criticizing myself; I am willing to let Elise's criticism of me roll off my back like water off a duck; I am willing to work in an organization that is fueled by appreciation.	I commit to using loving and kind self-talk; I commit to letting go of anyone else's criticism of me; I commit to creating an organization that is fueled by appreciation.
I am willing to prioritize and receive rest and relaxation each weekend.	I commit to prioritizing and receiving rest and relaxation each weekend.
I am willing to be more decisive myself; I am willing to work on a team where decisions get made.	I commit to making decisions that need and want to be made; I commit to creating a team norm where decisions get made in a sound and timely manner.
I am willing to stop micromanaging Molly.	I commit to creating conscious, clear agreements with Molly and fully communicating my requests to her.
I am willing to stop questioning my own judgment; I am willing to be unfazed by Chris's questioning of me; I am willing to work on a team where my experience is valued.	I commit to trusting my own wisdom; I commit to letting go of Chris's judgment of me; I commit to finding a team where my experience is valued.
I am willing to request a different supervisor; I am willing to report Brad to HR; I am willing to look for a different job at a different company; I am willing to organize with my colleagues to create a more just workplace.	I commit to finding a boss who is committed to justice and who treats me with respect.

I am willing to do everything in my power to create the conditions that result in 100,000 people being housed in the US.	I commit to cocreating the conditions that result in 100,000 people being housed in the US.

Here's one more hint about committing. It is important to phrase your commitment like this: I commit to _____. You don't want to say, "I am committing to . . ." or "I am committed to . . ." The words "I am committing" keep the commitment out in front of you. You will constantly *be committing* but never actually *commit*.

And the phrase "I am committed to . . ." implies that you are already doing something. You can truthfully say, "I am committed to brushing my teeth" because you've probably had a track record of brushing your teeth for years. It's not useful to say "I am committed to something" that you don't have a track record with because your subconscious mind will know you're lying to it, and it doesn't like that.

Finally, you will also want to frame your commitment in the positive. Your subconscious can only take orders in the affirmative. It can't *not* think of a chicken. Don't think of a chicken. Whoops! You just did! So it's better to commit *to* something versus *not to* something.

The difference may sound subtle, or just plain weird, but the way you word your commitment makes a huge difference in the amount of power it holds. Try saying the different versions out loud and see if you notice a difference for yourself.

The whole point of commitment is to get you off the bench and onto the playing field. Until you make a commitment, you're a spectator. Once you make that commitment, you're in the game for real. This is the threshold to cross, and on the other side, life becomes much more interesting and your work becomes much more impactful.

Are you ready to try this for yourself? Let's do it!

Act Now: Move from Wanting to Willing to Commitment

Think about an issue related to your work to repair the world that you want to explore further, then complete these sentences.

Related to my issue, I want . . . Allow yourself to express freely anything that comes to mind. No censorship or packaging it to be "appropriate" or "professional" or "realistic." Aim for the stars! _____

_____

_____

_____

_____

_____

Tune in to your own body and see if you are able to shift from wanting to being willing. If you are, continue to journal.

Regarding what I want, I am willing to . . . _____

_____

_____

_____

_____

_____

Tune in to your own body and see if a commitment is wanting to be made. If yes, articulate it like this:

I commit to . . . _____

_____

_____

_____

_____

_____

Remember to frame your commitment in the positive (being patient with my kids) rather than the negative (stop yelling at my kids).

Step in: Pick a spot on the ground to represent being all in with your commitment. When you feel ready, step into that spot, and declare your commitment out loud. See how it feels in your body to really own your commitment.

Celebration step: How will you celebrate your new commitment? Make sure it's something you can complete before the sun goes down today. _____

_____

_____

Regardless of your unconscious commitments, before you read any further, I want to invite you to consider making this conscious commitment out loud: I commit to contributing to repairing the world in a way that feeds my own aliveness and well-being.

Write it out in your own handwriting with any friendly amendments you want to add here: _____

_____

_____

_____

_____

Now that you've made this commitment, the final step is deciding what you are going to do about it. This is where you shift your focus from your inner work back to the outside world. This is where you introduce something different, off the Triangle and from your essence, aligned with what you really want, what you are willing to do, and your commitment. This is where the magic happens! _____

_____

_____

_____

_____

_____

Chapter 7 Takeaways

- Giving yourself permission to know and honor your yeses and your nos is an essential building block for being able to clarify your commitment.
- A yes is the alignment of your mind, body, and heart with any given possibility.
- A no is anything that is not a full-body yes.
- A commitment is an agreement between you and the universe. There are no other human beings required.
- Commitments are what set creating reality in motion.
- To clarify our commitment, we start with what we want, then what we are willing to do about it, and finally we see if a commitment emerges.
- You will stray from your path; making your big dent in the universe depends upon you being able to recommit again and again.

PART IV:
SHIFT YOUR CONTEXT

In the Hendricks Institute Leadership and Transformation program, we used to joke with one another that you're not really serious about doing the program until you've gotten a divorce, quit your job, or changed your name. Some people I know did all three! If things haven't been working for you, taking the steps in this section of the book might create some big changes for you. Be ready and have a safety net in place—or not. That's really your choice. Just know that this is straightforward stuff, but also a big deal.

You have put forth a lot of effort to get to this point in the process. You've faced what you've been avoiding. You've embraced your power. You've allowed yourself to feel your feelings and found the clarity on the other side, an initial sense of what you really want. By honoring your yeses and your nos, you've gotten out of limbo, refined what you want to the point where you are able to land on a commitment. Can we just take a minute and celebrate all your hard work with a round of high fives?

You've done so much inner exploration to get to this point. Now it's time to take your commitment out into the great big world and make some waves! It is from this grounded place of commitment that we go forth in the world to literally create reality. That's the real magic of being an effective change leader: creating a new reality. The game from here on out springs from commitments that you made and then recommitted to over and over again. The work never ends, but over time it gets easier and a lot more fun.

The next step is to shift your context.

Your context is how you organize yourself in body, mind, emotions, and spirit. Think of your context like a turtle's shell. It's your home that comes with you everywhere you go. So let's make it one that works for you. You can organize yourself unconsciously or consciously. I am a big proponent of the latter.

This section of the book is a menu of options for how you might proceed using your personal power to move in the direction of your commitment in a way that is authentic to you. The options can be selected à la carte or, if you really want to go for it, all together. Each of these options is a proven, effective, off-the-Drama-Triangle way to create reality. Think of them as invitations or provocations.

Here's what's on the menu:

- Appreciating: How can I shift my context to one of appreciation?
- Revealing: What has been hidden that now wants to be said?
- Agreeing: How can I create a context of healthy agreements?
- Contributing: How can I contribute from my genius?

By the way, these invitations are not only useful for navigating the complexity of leading social change. They're also good for building an entire life filled with love and purpose. But they're of limited use without the foundation of the inner work we did together in the first three parts of this book. As you integrate these context shifts into your leadership practice, you will be stepping into healthy responsibility and gaining a deepened sense of awareness of the complexity of connection across the web of life. Even though these may seem like micromoves, these are actually tendrils reaching out to build a macroweb of connections. In the same way that the smallest roots of one tree grow to make contact with roots from nearby trees and exchange information and nutrients, you will be shifting the context. Literally reweaving the web of life.

Ready? Let's dive in!

CHAPTER 8

SHIFTING FROM ENTITLEMENT TO APPRECIATION

Three times a year, we host the Billions Institute Fellows in our home in Claremont, California. During these retreats, we facilitate a group of social change leaders through our most advanced inner work. It takes a lot of courage to do this work and I am not above doing it myself. I'm right there with the fellows, learning and growing alongside them.

The warmth, camaraderie, and joy we experience when these coconspirators across a range of social justice and social change projects descend on our home is palpable. Most of the time, these retreats feel like a family reunion that only your favorite family members are invited to. One particular retreat, however, was veering off course.

Early in the morning, as the faculty team prepared for our third and final day together, I learned that some of the fellows had been complaining about their experience the day prior. Of course I was concerned by this. I want our fellows to be absolutely delighted, transformed, and transported by these retreats. But as I learned more about their complaints, I found myself feeling defensive and sinking into the Villain position on the Drama Triangle. My instinct was not only to defend myself and our faculty team but also, in true Judge Judy–persona fashion, to go on the offensive. My mind leapt into counterattack mode, with a barrage of blames and criticisms ready to level at our fellows.

And then, thank goodness, alarm bells went off in my brain and the words I had heard Kathlyn Hendricks speak so many times before came into my awareness. In that moment, I heard her ask, "How can you shift from entitlement to appreciation?"

And I stopped in my tracks.

You see, I felt entitled to our fellows loving and appreciating everything that I was doing. And I know that whenever I feel entitled about *anything*, it's time for me to shift from entitlement to appreciation. So right there in our morning faculty briefing, I said, "Hey y'all, I'm sensing that I'm veering into the territory of blame and criticism, and I'm hearing you may be, too. What if we shift into appreciation, right now? I'll go first . . ."

And though it took me a minute, I was able to come up with something I could appreciate. Then Nicole jumped in with her appreciation. Then Christine. Then Mike. Then Leslie. Then Susan. Before we knew it, we were laughing and enjoying ourselves, available for connection and creativity again, which was a good thing, because the fellowship meeting was about to start in a few minutes.

This context shift from entitlement to appreciation our faculty team had initiated together created such a profound effect on our state of mind that we decided to start off our fellowship meeting with the same invitation. As the fellows gathered around our living room that morning, I told them about what we had just experienced on the faculty team, shared an authentic appreciation in the moment, and invited them to join in with any appreciations that felt authentic to them.

Two hours later, every single one of our fellows had spoken an appreciation into the room. Through laughter. Through tears. Along the way, this new context of appreciation created an opening for powerful, authentic sharing among the group. The entire tone and context of our meeting shifted on a dime. Not just that morning. For good. The fellowship has been on a different trajectory ever since that day.

So, what are you appreciating right here, right now, exactly as it is?

Appreciation is not a replacement for facing your mistakes or making amends. It's not meant as a tactic for skipping over things or to avoid important conversations. Please don't interpret this to mean that if your employees are upset with how you are treating them you can demand a round of appreciations and everything will be just fine. No. We modeled appreciations by going first ourselves. We also made the effort to check in with fellows to make amends for any harm that had been done along the way of our learning and growth.

Appreciation isn't the soft stuff. Appreciation is also the hard stuff. Do you think it was easy for me in that moment to shift out of my own defensiveness and find something to appreciate? I promise you, it was not. Never underestimate the seduction of the Drama Triangle. Even for someone like me, who has been cultivating a discipline of appreciation for a decade, it took conscious effort. Years and years of practice with infusing appreciation into my daily life enabled me to facilitate that shift. With practice, you can do this, too.

Appreciation is one of the most powerful transformation moves available to you, and it doesn't require anyone else to do anything differently. You can do this one all by yourself. Cultivating this ability will make a huge difference in all your relationships, both personal and professional. So don't be afraid to be a solo appreciation artist. Your people will find you and soon enough you will get that band going.

So first ask yourself, Is there anywhere in my life where I feel entitled? How am I organizing myself to feel entitled? Where am I receiving blame or criticism? How am I dishing out blame or criticism to others?

These are not problems to solve. These are opportunities to shift the context. In this chapter, I'll show you how to begin the work of shifting into a state of appreciation. Let's start by unpacking what happens before we get there.

Eliminate the Blame and Criticism

I believe we slip into patterns of blame or criticism when we aren't able to catch ourselves in a state of entitlement quickly enough. If we are able to catch ourselves in time, in those early moments of feeling entitled, it is possible to prevent an outburst of criticism or blame. Entitlement is simply clinging hard to thinking that things should be a certain way. And if you can let go of needing life to be on your terms, if you can flow with what is and consciously direct your attention to what is working, then you get the benefit of that. What you appreciate, appreciates. It grows and grows, and you get more of that in your life.

If your entitlement progresses to the point where you are feeling the impulse to blame or criticize, you are in a persona. It's that simple. You feel afraid of something that's not yours to control. Your system is registering aversion and not taking time to face reality, tune in to what you really want, and isn't willing to become the source of that yourself without needing it from the outside. Well . . . queue the personas.

And you know what? Personas happen. So don't beat yourself up about it. But for heaven's sake, stop it as soon as possible. It will change your life and it will make you way more effective as a change leader. People might even start to like you and enjoy following you.

I can speak from my own experience that blame and criticism is my own personal go-to reaction when I'm feeling scared. Without a lot of conscious awareness, some quality time unwinding my personas, and a deliberate appreciation practice, I would be drowning in blame and criticism every single day. My brain is wired to notice what is wrong. Yours is, too. All of ours are or we wouldn't be here. Noticing what's wrong—up until now—has been helpful for the survival of our species. But too much attention to what is wrong is overkill and ultimately destructive for the thriving of people and teams.

A concrete example of a persona that shows up when I am feeling scared is my Woke White Lady. She constantly scans the environment for white people who are insufficient in their commitment to racial justice. She doesn't really like to call them out or call them in; rather, she prefers to bask in the knowledge that she is better than "those white people" from a comfortable distance. Woke White Lady is prepared at all times to blame and criticize all white people except herself and maybe a few select others. She might name-drop something to let you know that she's in the know or "doing the work." But the truth is Woke White Lady (a) isn't doing anything to make the world a better place (arguably she's making it worse), and (b) is a distraction from my own fears that I am utterly inadequate to the task of dismantling racism.

LaShawn Chatmon, executive director of the National Equity Project, reminds us that the real work of racial justice is done *in relationship, over time.* Nobody wants to be in relationship, over time, with my Woke White Lady persona. She is quite haughty.

When I notice Woke White Lady has come to work with me or is giving public comment at, say, a local school board meeting (as she does from time to time), I don't have to fix her. I simply have to give this persona some loving attention and ask her what she really wants. Underneath my blame and criticism, what I really want in my essence is to create a world where everyone can thrive and belong. Believing I'm better than anyone else (as my Woke White Lady persona believes) is antithetical to what I really want.

I am showing you my inner process here with noticing and shifting, one of many ways that I bring blame and criticism into my life. This process of turning inward can work for you, too. But sometimes people engage in blame and criticism because they are misinformed about what it takes to bring out the best in their people. Because how else will people improve if you don't at least give them some constructive criticism? How will people know when they've disappointed you? Or failed to live up to your expectations?

Well, you can give people all the information they need to learn and grow without an ounce of blame or criticism. It's called "speaking unarguably," and we will cover that more in chapter 9. But before we get to the next chapter, you can start right now by letting go of the notion that anybody, including yourself, is your improvement project. That isn't serving anybody. Instead, ask yourself this:

> What if my only job as a leader is to create a
> context in which everybody thrives?

Trust me. People are perfectly capable of improving without the slightest hint of blame or criticism. In fact, people flourish in a context of appreciation. So the first thing to do is disabuse yourself of the notion that blame or criticism has any place at all in your toolbox as a leader. They are evil twins; they are toxic for you and for those on the receiving end.

So if you feel entitled, notice that. Pay attention to what it is that "should" be different in the world. Notice where in your body you are registering that "should." Give yourself permission to feel your feelings and do some breathing and moving until you can get back into your prefrontal cortex and fully inhabit your body again. Then you become the source of what it is you "want" (read: "lack") in the world. Get skilled at noticing your sense of entitlement and doing this process before your brain turns to blame and criticism to distract you from what you're really feeling and what you really want. It's so much better for your health and your effectiveness to simply say, "Oh gosh, I just noticed I felt entitled for a minute there. I thought things *should* be like _____ and I realize that's not the case. It's not mine to control. I feel _____." Then redirect your attention to something you can appreciate in the moment. The more skilled you become in this process, the more you will become the source of that which is lacking in the world.

Generating Appreciation

Kathlyn Hendricks defines appreciation as "giving your sensitive awareness to something." I think of it as giving something or someone my undivided attention and presence. It's not fishing for compliments to dish out to others; it's noticing within myself what brings me a burst of joy, then saying it out loud.

Nobody ever died of too much appreciation, but I'm pretty sure there are some folks who have died prematurely from too much blame or criticism. You cannot possibly authentically appreciate someone too much. There is such a dearth of appreciation in our world. Every utterance of appreciation will feel like rain in the desert for most people. The key is it has to be sincere and specific.

A lot of people give cursory appreciation, like saying thank you when their assistant brings them coffee or replying to an email with the same. There's a difference between gratitude and appreciation. Thanking someone for something they did for you is great (and a given, I hope), but doing so is transactional—not transformational. We're going for transformational (versus transactional) leadership here!

Appreciation is making eye contact and communicating clearly exactly what you notice about someone's essence that is shining through and also the positive impact that has on you. It is a way of seeing someone without asking for anything in return. Here are some examples:

- "I noticed that you greet me each day with such kindness, and you really brighten my day. I feel so at home here. Thank you."
- "I noticed you've been working really late on getting ready for the big event, and I know it's a lot to manage. I just want you to know that I see your dedication and commitment to this organization, and it feels so good to me to know that I have a real partner in you."
- "I know what you just did was hard for you, and I see you struggling to do the work, and I appreciate your determination!"

The key is that you're not treating someone as a means to your ends. You're not thanking them for something they do *for you*; you're noticing them for *who they are*.

One more thing: don't forget to include yourself in your new appreciation habit. Is there anything you blame or criticize yourself for? What could you appreciate about yourself instead? While appreciating yourself isn't a magical unicorn hat that you can wear to fend off blame or criticism, it is something you can generate internally without needing anyone's permission or assistance. It is a good way to fill your own cup so you're less thirsty for outside approval in the first place.

How to Create a Context of Appreciation with Your Team

I started off this chapter with a story about the power of appreciation to shift a group from blame and criticism. Ideally, we don't let things spiral to the point where an intervention is necessary. Appreciation is something you can lead with, all the time. At the Billions Institute, we begin every Monday meeting with each person on the team being invited to share one appreciation.

Some of my most cherished memories from leading the 100,000 Homes Campaign are from our appreciation dinners. Since we lived in six different cities, we were only able to be together in person as a full team three or four times a year. Twice a year, we held our team retreats at a spacious ranch in rural Colorado that was forty-five minutes away from the nearest grocery store. So we'd do a massive grocery run on the way out, then take turns preparing meals and sharing responsibilities around the house. At each retreat, one of our dinners was designated an "appreciation dinner." Shortly after we sat down, one person would start it off with an appreciation of one other person on the team. It was always heartfelt and sincere. Then another person would go. Then another. There was no requirement for reciprocity. No limit to how many times you could share. Just seeing and acknowledging and appreciating one another. Always laughter. And always tears. It usually went on for at least an hour, and every time we did this, I thought my heart was going to burst. Jake Maguire used to proudly claim, "This team would bleed for one another!" I believe he was right, and I believe appreciation was the fuel behind that bond.

Cultivating a habit of appreciation (both noticing what brings you happiness and expressing it out loud to somebody) is number one on the "shift your context" menu because you can do it all by yourself and it is such a high-leverage move. This is especially true when you are experiencing blame and criticism, regardless of whether you are generating the blame and criticism or are on the receiving end of it. You can't go wrong with using your personal power to introduce some appreciation into the mix. It's not about being a Pollyanna and not noticing the entitlement; it's about depriving the entitlement, blame, and criticism of the oxygen they need to survive. Just simply putting your attention elsewhere. It's not a magic cure-all. Your environment may be so toxic that you ultimately decide to leave, but give this a try for at least a month and see if anything is different before you give notice.[6]

Act Now: Move from Entitlement to Appreciation

Think about an area in your life where things aren't working out the way they "should." What do you feel entitled to? How do you think it "should" be? Go ahead and give yourself a minute or two to speak or write from a discovery about what's wrong and how things "should" be. _____

_____

_____

_____

_____

_____

_____

_____

_____

6. If you would like to receive an email every day for thirty days with an appreciation prompt to support you in developing this new habit, sign up at www.billionsinstitute.com/appreciation-challenge.

Did you get it all out? If not—keep going! Come back when you've gotten it all out.

Now complete this sentence:

When I tune in to _____ [the problem], I feel entitled to_____ [how things "should" be].

Good job! You've stated something unarguable!

Now consciously shift your attention to find and notice anything that you can appreciate about the way things are exactly right here, right now. Give *that* your attention.

Once you are feeling yourself back in your body and your creative brain, one thing you might ask yourself is, "How can I become a source of what I most want in the world?"

Chapter 8 Takeaways

- Consciously creating a context of appreciation is the foundation upon which all transformation rides.
- Appreciation is the antidote to entitlement, blame, and criticism.
- Are you feeling entitled to anything? Appreciate life just as it is in this moment.
- Are you feeling blamed or criticized? Appreciate yourself. Then read the next chapter to determine what, if anything, you want to reveal to the person blaming or criticizing you.
- Are you blaming or criticizing anyone? Appreciate something about them instead.
- Don't forget to include yourself in the habit of appreciation.

CHAPTER 9

SHIFTING FROM CONCEALING TO REVEALING

When I was leading the 100,000 Homes Campaign, I received a phone call from a trusted colleague who informed me that a prominent national leader in homelessness had spoken dismissively about our work. Apparently, when asked about our campaign, their response was "Well, it's a good *marketing* campaign . . ." As if we were simply making things look good!

When I heard about this, I felt my blood boil with anger and my stomach clench with fear. I felt angry because I knew that they knew darn well we weren't just *talking* about what needed to be done. We were working shoulder to shoulder with communities to *do* what needed to be done. It seemed unfair to me that they would use their position and privilege to undermine our efforts. So their passive-aggressive criticism percolated in my awareness for a solid month or two. I also felt scared. This person was influential in our field, and I knew all too well how easy it was for community leaders to punt on making the hard decision to work with our campaign. I was afraid that their characterization of our campaign would be all the excuse a community leader would need to abandon the difficult challenge we were inviting them to embrace.

I'm ashamed to admit that, for a couple of days, I spent just as much time scheming how to out-maneuver this person as I did focusing on how I could help more communities house more people more quickly, a.k.a. my job. And after all that inner monologuing, I never said anything to this person about it. Ever. Even to this day! I chose to conceal my feelings rather than to reveal them, and in so doing I missed my opportunity to shift the context.

When you conceal important information from a relevant party, it puts in motion a pattern I learned about in my apprenticeship with Kathlyn Hendricks called Withhold, Withdraw, Project. When you withhold the communication, you unconsciously withdraw from the relationship, and then project onto that person something that is actually true about yourself. I've seen it happen far too many times in my own life to question this pattern. And the Withhold, Withdraw, Project pattern does absolutely nothing to make the world a better place.

We'll never know what might have happened had I shifted the context by choosing revealing over concealing. Imagine for a minute what might have happened in the same scenario if I had chosen to do my inner work more thoroughly.

If I had done an instant replay of my bodily sensations, I would have realized my stomach felt clenched, and I'd have said to my friend, "Oh gosh, I feel afraid that the people whom they said that to will use it as an excuse to avoid doing the hard work of our campaign."

Right after my fear, I'd notice a wave of anger, a sense of a boundary having been crossed. I'd notice I was getting something I didn't want on behalf of the campaign, which was unsolicited criticism and gossip. Then I'd realize that I was caught in the Withhold, Withdraw, Project cycle and consider giving them a call.

The stakes feel high because this person is a truly prominent national figure who has far more positional and societal power than I do. If I mess up this conversation, it could set our efforts back even further. So I might go for a little walk or do some breathing exercises or even ask my partner, boss, or colleagues to be a sounding board for me. But once I've felt my feelings and gotten clear on what I really want, and what I am committed to (assisting communities to help 100,000 people from the streets into housing), I would give them a call.

Here's what I might have said: "I heard that you had called our campaign a good 'marketing' campaign. I feel sad and angry that you said that. I've made up a story that you are enabling communities to avoid doing the hard work of housing people who were living on the streets. I've also made up the story that you are undermining our work. These are just stories that I've made up without checking in with you, and I realized maybe I'm missing some important information. Would you be willing to shed some light on where you're coming from here?"

I might have asked them, "Are you willing to cut it out?" and they may have said, "Actually, no, I am not, because I have a different commitment that's counter to yours." Well, at least then I'd know. Sometimes you don't get the change you want in the world. Think of it like going to the gym. With each workout of your integrity muscles, you become more ready for the next big challenge.

It's impossible to know how it would have played out. They could have gotten defensive and denied having said it, or genuinely apologized to me, saying, "Gosh, I really thought it was a marketing campaign. You mean the communities have already moved 45,000 people from the streets into housing? My goodness, that is brilliant! Thank you for clarifying that!" (Unlikely.)

While I cannot know how they would have reacted or responded, what I do know is this: They'd have learned that they can't talk shit about us without it getting back to us. They'd have had the opportunity to receive feedback on the consequences of their actions. They'd have learned that I was the kind of leader who had the courage to give them the chance to clarify what they had said if there was a misunderstanding.

Here's one more thing I know for sure: If I had pursued the strategy outlined in the do-over version, speaking unarguably, choosing revealing over concealing, I would have fully leveraged my personal power. I'd have stepped more fully into healthy responsibility for the situation. I'd have gotten off the Drama Triangle. I would have been the kind of leader I hope I now am.

Concealing happens all the time. Many of us were socialized to be polite at the expense of being authentic. Remember this classic: "If you can't say something nice, say nothing"? *Concealing* is exactly what it sounds like: You are saying nothing. You are holding in or hiding important information.

Likewise, many of us were socialized to conceal our truth from others. Some of us, especially those of us who have experienced marginalization in our lives, have received all too much pushback that our truth is not welcome here. Even worse, that it's not safe for us to speak freely. This socialization is pervasive, it's real, and it serves to keep the oppressive patterns going.

While not without its risks, revealing holds the potential to shift this context. *Revealing* simply means disclosing important information to affected parties. Doing so effectively occurs when what you say both in words and in body language is in alignment with your truth. When you choose to reveal, you use your personal power to shift the context in ways that are far more powerful than making yourself small or going with the flow.

In this chapter, we'll dig into the ramifications of concealing and come up with some tangible ways to get more comfortable with revealing your inner emotions and feelings.

Speaking Unarguably

The simplest way to get started with revealing is to say something that cannot be argued with. And there are only so many things you can say that can't be argued with, so let's get those categories out there first. No one can argue with us if these are the things we speak about:

- Body sensations (I have butterflies in my stomach.)
- Feelings (I feel scared.)
- Thoughts (This reminds me of something that happened in third grade.)
- Requests (Would you be willing to . . . ?)

I should say that no one *should* argue with you if you speak about those things. The shocking thing is people sometimes do, and as a parent I'm embarrassed to admit I know where it all starts.

Kid: I feel scared.

Me: There's nothing to be afraid of.

Kid: I'd really like a glass of water.

Me: It's too late for you to be thirsty. You'll pee in the bed.

We may say something unarguable, and someone attempts to deny our reality. That's the definition of "gaslighting." If anyone tries to argue with us about our body sensations, our feelings, our thoughts, or our wants, it's not helpful to stay in the details. Telescope the conversation out and talk about the bigger picture, as in, "I noticed I said something one would think is unarguable—that I felt sad—and you said I didn't feel sad. Houston, we have a problem."

The key to speaking unarguably is to dig down to get to the kernel of that which cannot be argued with. Sometimes we stop short of going all the way to it, and that's where we can inadvertently blame and criticize. Keep going until it is something about you (not them).

Speaking unarguably is contagious and aligns you (and anyone in your sphere) to what is. To reality. To the present moment. Speaking unarguably about the little things is seemingly minor but has an outsized impact. It takes courage to decide to reveal, but once you commit, it's actually quite simple to execute.

Final Check Before Revealing

Before you go off revealing to people willy-nilly, ask yourself if you want to be in relationship with the person you intend to reveal something to. Revealing, even though it may be painful for others to hear or poorly received, creates the possibility for authentic connection. If you don't want to be closer to the other parties involved, don't do it. I have noticed personally that sometimes I say I don't want to be closer to somebody, but that's really just a way to chicken out on my aliveness. Only you know what's true for you. Like everything, the choice is yours.

Regardless of what you decide, know that revealing is always a gift, both for you and the other person. For you, this will open your energy, fuel your aliveness, and build your empowerment muscles. For the other person, what you offer is both information they would not otherwise have access to and, if you do it well, an invitation into deeper relationship with you. Even if you say something they don't like or want to hear. Even if you make a mistake (and most of us do), you are creating an opening. And that's OK, because, as my friend Dr. Michelle Pledger likes to say, practice precedes progress.

Likewise, remember that if someone has the courage to reveal something authentic and unarguable to you, that is a gift, too. Receive it as such. Even if it stings. Even if it reinforces your biggest fear about yourself. Kathlyn Hendricks calls this "appreciating the messenger regardless of the delivery." If you are in any trusted position of leadership, I want to encourage you to get really good at this.

Step-by-Step Guide to Revealing

Below are some guidelines for revealing in a way that is most likely to be effective:

1. Check yourself. What aspects of your identity and power will help or hinder connection with the other person? What are your intentions? To create connection and share something that is true about you with the intention that it will be of service to your work to make the world a better place? Or a hit-and-run to get it off your chest? Only proceed if your answer is to create connection. If it is to score a point, do a Persona Interview (appendix B) with the persona that believes this is a good idea. Then come back later when you're in your essence.

2. Ask the other person if they are available for connection. This allows the other person to check into their own emotional and psychic state and decide whether or not now is a good time. You might ask, "Are you available for me to share something important with you?" or "Is now a good time for us to talk?"

3. Wait to see what they say. Listen not only to their words, but also observe their body language. Assess whether or not they are truly available to receive what you want to share. Remember your work on knowing your yeses and nos? Extend this grace to others. Wait until you hear a definite yes.

4. Timing matters. Find a time for connection that is unhurried and spacious. Anytime you're rushing or hurrying, you're inevitably in the gravitational pull of the Drama Triangle. So don't do it until you and the other person are able to speak without needing to rush.

5. When you do talk, share something about yourself and something that cannot be argued with. This is what therapists are talking about when they encourage couples to use "I" statements. But I've found people screw that up, too, saying something like "I feel like you're a terrible person" and then saying, "What?! I used an 'I' statement!"

6. Appreciate the other person for listening to you.

7. Stop talking. Listen and remain open to what you might learn. It's OK at this point for you to allow some uncomfortable silence. Remember that you had time to prepare for this and the other person may be hearing this for the first time. They may need time to think, process, and reconnect later. Leave space for alternative experiences, different viewpoints, and complexity. The person who can

endure the longest uncomfortable silence almost always wins. By "winning" I mean they create the greatest opening for transformation.

8. Appreciate yourself for revealing. Do not skip this step. Do a little happy dance. Give yourself a high five. Whatever way you want to reinforce to your consciousness the aliveness you feel, do it!

Revealing in Context: Specific Scenarios

What follows are some specific scenarios that I've seen show up in social change contexts that you might want to try on for size:

> **If you catch yourself blaming or criticizing yourself or someone else, correct it immediately.** Out loud. Say to yourself or the other person, "Oh my gosh, I just realized I was criticizing you a minute ago. I think I might be scared about _____. I apologize for criticizing you." How *amazing* would it be if someone who had just blamed or criticized you said that to you, right? So instead of hoping the clue bird will land on other people, you can just start doing it yourself and with any luck it will be contagious to your colleagues, too.

> **If somebody blames or criticizes you, you can simply communicate a body sensation.** "Oh wow. When you said that, I noticed I stopped breathing for a minute." Just that burst of authenticity is feedback to the other person and might jolt them back into more authentic connection.

If somebody seems unwilling to make a deci-sion, make a request. "Would you be willing to let us know how you want that decision to be made by the time our team meets again next Tuesday?" Clear, simple, direct requests are exceedingly rare in most organizations that I've known. They go like this: "Would you be willing to . . . [fill in the blank with exactly what you want]?" followed by complete silence and giving the other person the space and grace to say yes or no.

If you are micromanaging somebody, you could interrupt that pattern with a reveal. It could go something like this: "I've noticed that I am nitpicking your decisions left and right, and what I really want is for you to fully own this process from start to finish without any involvement from me. Can we sit down for an hour later today so I can give you all my guid-ance and answer all your questions, and after that it is yours?"

And if you are being micromanaged, you could interrupt that pattern with a simple reveal about your body sensations and what you want. "I noticed I closed down a little bit there, and I had the thought that I'll never be good at this. And I really want to do this part of my job incredibly well, and I feel afraid that I will never please you. Can we talk about your experience of this?"

Act Now: Move from Concealing to Revealing

Moving from concealing to revealing is less about the outcome of your revealing and more about the aliveness you will gain from doing so. If you get a no in response to your reveal, at least now you know. Let's explore what you might want to reveal next. Ask yourself some questions:

Who have I withheld communication from? _____

_____

_____

What have I not told them? _____

_____

_____

What am I afraid they will say or do? _____

_____

_____

Use the unarguable speaking questions below to decide exactly what it is you might reveal to them in your next conversation. Related to the information you've been withholding, ask yourself these questions:

Are there any body sensations that come up for me? What's happening where? _____

_____

_____

Are there any feelings or emotions I'd like to express? _____

_____

_____

What thoughts come up for me? _____
_____
_____

Do I have any requests? What are they? (Remember to start
with "Would you be willing to . . .") _____
_____
_____

Schedule the conversation. Choose a time that is desirable
for you and make the request.

Chapter 9 Takeaways

- Concealing is withholding important information
  from an affected party.
- Revealing is disclosing important information to
  an affected party.
- Revealing, though not without risk, creates the
  possibility for transformation. It is an incredibly
  powerful shift move.
- Only reveal to people you want to be closer to,
  because that will inevitably happen, even if you do
  it wrong.
- Speaking unarguably means restricting your
  reveal to things that cannot be argued with,
  namely, your body sensations, your emotions,
  your thoughts, and your requests.

CHAPTER 10

MAKING HEALTHY AGREEMENTS

Nothing puts more sand in the gears of social change than poor agreements. If there was one chapter I could mark with a giant yellow highlighter, it would be this one. Stick with me and I'll show you how to generate healthy, life-giving agreements so you and your team can thrive.

Remember our friend Eunice from chapter 3? She switched from part-time to full-time work to run the Gen2Gen campaign for Encore.org and in doing so realized she had stretched herself too thin between work and home. I know many of us can relate.

Eunice discovered that some of the agreements that used to work for her no longer did. Namely the implicit agreement that she would now spend two hours each day commuting, that she would promptly answer 100 percent of her emails, and that she would continue to be the primary coordinator of the kids' activities and family dinners. Something had to change, or Eunice was going to flame out.

And she nearly did, until she changed a couple of key agreements with the most important people in her life, using the formula we share at the end of this chapter. And what a difference it made.

She changed an agreement with her colleagues that enabled her to telecommute all but one day each month, freeing up two hours per day.

She changed an agreement with herself that she would no longer answer 100 percent of her emails. Somehow Eunice had internalized that she needed to answer every single email that was sent to her on some stringent (but made-up) time-table. Says who, right? But this is a great example of how an implicit agreement with oneself can be really powerful. When Eunice made the implicit explicit, then reconsidered it in light of her own commitment and priorities, she was able to let go of the "should" (note the Villain persona signature word here) she was holding on to about answering 100 percent of her emails. Turns out Eunice's guilt about breaking her self-imposed "should" about email was an even bigger drain on her energy than answering every single email. But in changing this agreement with herself, Eunice freed up all that energy for more creative pursuits. And thus far, nobody seems to have been harmed by an unanswered email.

Eunice also made a new agreement with her husband that he would be responsible for dinner three nights a week. In return, she agreed that she would refrain from complaining and be thrilled by whatever was on the menu, even if that meant ordering takeout three nights in a row.

Things are working really well for Eunice now. They can for you, too, by creating healthy agreements. Here's the deal: you can't make big, bold change in the world without other people joining you for the cause. It's too much for you to do by yourself. And the number-one thing that will sabotage your team and your efforts is poor agreements. Teams that make big, bold change in the world are built one healthy agreement at a time.

The good news is it's not that hard, actually, to create healthy agreements. In this chapter, I'm going to break that down for you and show you how. Like many concepts in this book, the ability to make healthy agreements is something that I refined during my two-year apprenticeship with the Hendricks Institute.

Explicit and Implicit Agreements

Let's start with two basic kinds of agreements: explicit and implicit. In the US, we drive on the right side of the road; in the UK, people drive on the left side of the road. These are explicit agreements because they're codified in motor vehicle laws. Other examples of explicit agreements might be an employee manual or the scope of work in a contract. Explicit agreements are out in the open and available for everyone to easily find and interpret.

But how many miles over the speed limit can you drive without getting a ticket? That one is not as obvious and it's definitely not written down anywhere. In some places, whether or not you get stopped by the police or get a ticket has nothing to do with how fast you were driving and everything to do with your race or social status. Sometimes when I'm in an unfamiliar city, I defer to how fast the locals are driving by keeping up with the traffic. As long as I'm driving safely, I assume I will not get a ticket, even if I'm going a little bit over the posted speed limit. Is that because I'm a white woman or because it's generally accepted to drive five miles over the posted speed limit? It's almost impossible for me to know. That's an implicit agreement. They're a lot trickier to navigate and change.

We enter into explicit and implicit agreements all the time. They're necessary if groups of people are to cooperate in our society and on our teams. And when they're working well, we experience a lot of harmony and ease. When they're off kilter, everything is out of sorts. So let's do this right for both explicit and implicit agreements.

The first step is to make implicit agreements explicit. To use the skill of speaking unarguably from the last chapter and state without any judgment, "I've assumed that an unwritten rule around here is that we work on weekends. Did I get that right?"

Then, once everything is out in the open, the next step is to apply the principles for healthy agreements to get things on track.

Principles for Healthy Agreements

Here are four principles for healthy agreements:

1. Only say yes to things you actually want to do.
2. Say no to things you don't want to do.
3. Do the things you agreed to do, on time, without needing to be reminded.
4. If an agreement isn't working for you any longer, proactively change it.

When I learned about these principles at the Hendricks Institute, I shared them with my team on the 100,000 Homes Campaign. Over time they became our operating norms. My role within the team was to be a sounding board, to support the team as a whole and each member individually to make good decisions and grow through challenges. My role was not to follow up on them to make sure they did what they said they were going to do. I was adamant that I was unwilling to supervise anyone in the traditional sense of that word. That's junior varsity, I told them. And this team is varsity!

Think about how much time is wasted as a supervisor by checking up on whether or not someone did what they said they were going to do. We created an explicit agreement that we would do what we said we'd do and proactively change agreements if they weren't working. I didn't have to waste any energy at all following up to see if people accomplished what they said they would because they did it or they came to the team and said, "Hey, I'm falling a little behind on this one." All our creativity was freed up to devote to helping communities get people off the streets and into housing. I also endeavored to create a context where people on the team didn't feel accountable to me. I wanted them to feel accountable to the mission and to one another. I think for the most part the team pulled that off!

One thing you might consider doing right now is deciding that you are a leader who creates a context for healthy agreements within your teams or organizations. This can also work for your family. Maybe you could even make a new commitment and put that new skill to work: "I commit to making healthy agreements in every aspect of my life." Let's dig a little deeper into these four principles of healthy agreements.

Only Say Yes to What You Actually Want to Do

Knowing your yeses and nos is a prerequisite for healthy agreements. (See chapter 7 for a refresher on knowing yeses and nos.) The tricky thing is that sometimes you need a little bit of time and space to be able to fully tune in to your own body wisdom.

It might be some time before everyone in the world has read this book and knows to say, when they make a request, "Please take your time and know that your no is as good as your yes to me."

One technique I use to create that room for my own inner wisdom to surface is to say something like, "Oh, that's an interesting idea. Thank you for thinking of me. Can I sleep on that and get back to you with a decision tomorrow?" If I don't feel a full-body yes immediately, that buys me twenty-four hours and some space away from people to tap into my own authentic yes or no.

When you only say yes to what you actually want to do, you will have way less stress in your life. You will be known as someone who can be trusted because you're being honest with yourself and others about your bandwidth. Through your example, you may even inspire others to give themselves permission to do the same.

If you have that full-body yes, either immediately or upon further exploration, by all means communicate that yes and then be sure to write it down so you will remember what you have agreed to, including the due date. Then your job is simply to do what you said you'd do. Easy, right? But what if you don't have a full-body yes to someone's request?

Say No to What You Don't Want to Do

Before we go any further, take a minute and think about how liberating it was for you to get clear on your actual nos in chapter 7. That felt good, right?

Now you're venturing out into new territory: not just knowing your no, but actually *saying* your no to other people who may or may not want for you what you want for yourself. Brace yourself. This is where it gets interesting.

I once allowed two of my friends to stay in my home for the weekend so they could save money on a hotel. My wife and I were leaving town early the next morning. We had arranged for a dog sitter to pick up our two pugs around 9:00 or 10:00 a.m. As we were saying good night—and I knew I would be gone before they woke up—I casually asked one of them if they would be willing to take the dogs out for a quick walk if they got up early to get coffee.

And my friend sighed and said, "As I imagine walking your dog, I think about the likelihood that they'll poop, and I know I'd have a baggie, but I really don't want excrement near my hands. So, no. I'm not willing to walk your dogs."

I was livid. "I'm saving you hundreds of dollars letting you stay in my place, and you can't even walk my freaking dogs?!? Are you kidding me? How can you be so *selfish*?" *Ooh!* I was so angry with them at the time! But they insisted it was a no to walking my dogs.

Now before you get on the Drama Triangle with me and my friend here, let me bring out the slow-motion instant-replay camera. Was I entitled to having my dogs walked even though I was letting them stay? No. I was not. We had no such agreement.

When they had asked me if they could stay, I very easily could have said, "Oh, I'd love to host you. In exchange, though, I have a request as well: Would you be willing to walk my dogs briefly the next morning?" But I had already agreed to host them with no reciprocal request.

I was coming at this from a place of entitlement (versus appreciation). The primary problem was not that they weren't willing to walk my dogs. I felt entitled to them returning a favor, and that was the first cause of my upset.

It's really important to listen to, and honor, another person's no. Otherwise we're relying upon power-over and oppression to get things done in the world. For the rest of my life I will remember this fabulous example of someone completely unfazed by communicating their no. Even though I was super irritated, it was a real gift.

That said, I also get to choose whom I want to be in close relationship with, and though I am still on very good terms with the person in this story because we were both completely honest with one another and didn't hold anything back, I don't go out of my way to seek them out. I choose to invest my energy in relationships with people who are slightly more agreeable in general. And that's all OK. We all get to decide whom we want to work with and play with.

I am already anticipating the "yeah, buts" to this statement. "Not everybody gets to decide whom they want to work with. We don't all have that amount of privilege, Becky." But hear me out on this one. The intended audience for this book is people who work in the nonprofit sector in the United States. That's one out of every ten jobs. So while you may not be able to leave a toxic environment easily or immediately, I know in my bones it's possible. If that is your situation, I will hold tight to that possibility while you sort it out.

Everybody gets to have their no. Everybody.

If we repeatedly have a no to doing our jobs, it's likely that at some point our employer will have a no to keeping us on the payroll. That's an extreme example, but most of the time the results of giving someone the space and grace to have their no are far less dramatic. I just want to put the most extreme possibilities out there, because we can now set that aside as ridiculous.

I think sometimes people hold themselves back from expressing their no because they're afraid it will end the relationship, or they'll get fired. And that could happen. But only if the relationship wasn't worth maintaining in the first place. In most cases, it's possible to express your truth *and* maintain the relationship. In fact, I believe that speaking your truth is the only thing that makes a healthy relationship possible at work or in your personal life.

So, this isn't about saying, "No, and by the way, screw you!" This is more like "I realized that I don't actually want to walk your dogs, and I care about you, and I'd love to be helpful in figuring out how everyone can get what they need."

With this skill of knowing and expressing your no, you may be the odd one out for a while. With any luck, your clarity and maturity will resonate with other people and they will begin to mimic your approach. This is how you address the underlying causes of dysfunction and oppression. Your healthy agreements can ripple out and support others in being more effective and healthier, too. Not that that's why you do it, but it's a nice side benefit.

Do the Things You Agreed to Do, On Time, Without Needing to be Reminded

A quick note for people with societal or positional power: you might get away with more broken agreements than you're even consciously aware of because your colleagues will be reluctant to hold you accountable, which at first might seem like a perk of being the boss. The problem is that you have a disproportionate impact on the leadership tone and context of your organization. So if you're sucky at agreements, you're tacitly giving everyone else permission to be, too. It's all the more important for you to publicly hold yourself accountable for keeping the agreements you make. So please read this section closely and assume you're guilty.

Not keeping the agreements that we make creates a massive energy leak, and we need all our energy going to more important things, like actually repairing the world.

When you break agreements with yourself and others, part of your brain's attention is taken up with reminding yourself that you didn't do that thing you said you'd do (even when you're not conscious of it). Another bit of your attention is probably making you feel guilty for not doing the thing you "should" have done.

This might be bearable if only one member of the team had only one broken agreement, but a lot of teams I've known operate with many members of the team routinely breaking many explicit and implicit agreements.

There are three big reasons you may not always keep your agreements:

1. You didn't want to make the agreement in the first place.
2. You don't have a functioning system to keep track of your agreements.
3. You didn't actually agree.

If you didn't want to make the agreement in the first place, cut it out. Don't agree to anything you don't actually want to do. Go back and proactively change the agreement.

If you don't have a functioning system to keep track of your agreements, make one now. It's too hard to keep track of all your agreements in your head, so don't try. You could create an agreements notebook, start a Google Docs file, or use an app like Things or Trello. As you and others complete your agreements, check them off and celebrate!

Something you might want to consider after everyone on your team has read this chapter is putting time on the schedule to ask, "What are our implicit agreements? And are they actually working for all of us?"

If things are working for you and your team, that's great. For the things that don't, you can ask directly to change those agreements. Organizations run on agreements. Teams run on agreements. Changing the world requires healthy agreements. If you can get this right, it will free up vast stores of energy and creativity to put toward actually doing the work.

Act Now: Agreements Inventory

What were your three biggest yeses from chapter 7? Are there any agreements you want to change in your life to create room for those three yeses to come to fruition? List them here: _____

_____
_____
_____
_____
_____

What were your three biggest nos from chapter 7? Are you overriding them in any way? Do any agreements need to be changed so that you can fully honor these nos of yours? _____

_____
_____
_____
_____
_____

Have you said yes to anything you don't actually want to do? List those agreements here: _____

_____
_____
_____
_____
_____

Are there any agreements you've made that you aren't keeping?
You said you would do something, and you haven't done it on
time? Or you said you wouldn't do something, and you did it
anyway? List them here: _____

_____

_____

_____

_____

_____

Put a star next to any agreement that you'd like to proactively
change and do so using the steps outlined below.

Change Agreements That Aren't Working for You

This is perhaps the single greatest shift move of all: the ability
to proactively change agreements that no longer work for you.
Having completed the agreements inventory above, you now
know what they are. The question is, What are you going to do
about it?

I've had the privilege of witnessing some people do a truly
fantastic job of proactively changing agreements, and I want
to share a proven formula for changing agreements with you
here. You can use this by inserting what you want to say under
each heading.

1. **Acknowledge the original agreement.** I realize
   that I agreed to present the findings from my report
   at next week's staff meeting.
2. **Reveal what's changed for you and state what
   you are now willing to agree to. Do not use this
   step to make excuses. You are not negotiating
   or asking for permission. You are stating a fact,**

what you are willing to agree to. I'm looking at my schedule for this week and realizing that the soonest I can complete this is the following Wednesday.

3. **Express respect and regard for the other person and create space for them to express what is true for them.** I care about how this will affect you and welcome your thoughts and feedback for me.

4. **Request confirmation and make room for their yeses and nos.** Will this work for you if I get it to you by Wednesday at 2:00 p.m.?

5. **Express appreciation.** I really appreciate how flexible you are with me. It helps me bring my best to this team. Thank you.

So, what are you waiting for? Go on and proactively change any agreements that aren't working for you anymore! You're going to feel so liberated once you do! And it will free up tons of energy for the work you are most here to do. Good luck!

Chapter 10 Takeaways

• Only say yes to things you actually want to do.
• Say no to things you don't want to do.
• Do the things you said you'd do, on time, without needing to be reminded.
• Proactively change agreements that no longer work for you.

CHAPTER 11

CONTRIBUTING FROM YOUR GENIUS

One of the most liberating and impactful ways you can shift the context is to commit to living in and contributing from your unique genius. People who work in the social sector are wildly creative, because in most cases we are literally making something from nothing. We create new ways of being, doing, and interacting that didn't exist before.

Think of your work as your canvas. With everything you say and do, you are creating something new in the world. Your art may not be as tangible as making a jewelry box out of papier-mâché but it's just as creative. You are "a creative" whether you think of yourself as one or not.

And nothing will burn out a creative more quickly than not having a clear way to express that creativity. If you are not spending at least 50 percent of your time doing things you love that you're really good at, and that bring you joy and satisfaction just for the sake of doing them, then you are not going to feel fulfilled. This is the final frontier of shifting the context. It's a way to get off the Drama Triangle big-time and dispense forever with notions about what you "should" be doing.

In our seminars, we call the experience of doing what you love and you're really good at being "in your genius." We got this term from Gay and Kathlyn Hendricks (if you want to learn more, read *The Big Leap* or *The Genius Zone* by Gay Hendricks). In his book *Flow*, Mihály Csíkszentmihályi calls it being in a state of "flow." The Japanese concept of *ikigai*, finding joy through a meaningful purpose in life (a combination of what you love, what the world needs, what you can be paid for, and what you are good at) points to the same thing. Jim Collins calls it the Hedgehog Concept in his book *Good to Great*. No matter what you call it, it is a combination of what you are deeply passionate about, what you are really good at, and what fuels your aliveness.

Being in your genius can be manifested both in *what* you do and *how* you go about doing it. An example of a zone of genius for me is delivering keynote addresses. I'm really good at them and people seem to really appreciate them. But when I dig a little deeper and look at not just what I'm doing but how I do it, I start to discover clues to my genius. When I'm preparing my remarks, I consciously put myself in the audience and ask, "What does this group of people need and want to hear?" And I stay in a place of wondering until ideas come to me. When they do, I can actually feel it in my body, like a thud, like a gymnast landing a dismount. I just *know*, and it's not a result of effort—it's a result of relaxing. This is the genius quality of receiving and allowing.

Then, as I'm actually delivering the keynote, I am right in the flow of the moment. Words seem to move through me, and I feel completely at ease, even in front of thousands of people. These are the genius qualities of allowing and spontaneity.

Your genius will have similar layers and levels of nuance. The more familiar you are with your own ways of being in your genius, the more you can incorporate them into your work. That may take the form of changing your actual job description so you can let go of things that aren't in your genius and make room for things that are. Or, it could involve doing the same things, just differently. You get to play with that.

The way you know you are in your genius is that you feel more alive, more energized, and more engaged in life. It's also likely that you are having so much fun that you feel like you're getting away with something. You may feel a little bit guilty that you're getting paid to do what you're doing. Don't worry about this because, in fact, you *should* be getting paid to do it. In fact, you should be getting paid lots of money to do it, because it's true genius. The results are great for everyone. Everybody wins when we show up in our genius.

Many people mistakenly believe their work needs to involve suffering for them to deserve a reward (such as being paid). I don't believe that for a minute. If I could wave a magic wand, everyone would be contributing to all the good things they want to happen in the world from their zone of genius, all the time.

In this chapter, we'll develop a clearer picture of how your particular genius fits into the bigger picture of social change, and how you can get (and stay) in your zone of genius for the greater good.

Some Not-So-Genius Ways We Get Stuck

There are three other zones you can be in when you're not in your zone of genius. They are the zones of excellence, competence, and incompetence.

When you're in your "zone of excellence," you're doing something you're really good at that other people appreciate.

Maybe you get paid really well or rewarded in some other way for doing it. But it doesn't bring you an inner sense of joy. You don't feel more alive after doing it, and most likely you feel somewhat drained. This is where most people get stuck, because there's often a lot of incentive to stay here.

Your "zone of competence" is an area of your work where there are other people who are just as good as you, and you really have to put a lot of effort into making sure things go well. It's OK to do things in your zone of competence. Most of us probably do a lot of the time. It's just that we're not going to feel that sense of flow.

Last but not least is your "zone of incompetence." This is pretty obvious: it's the realm of things that you are not very good at. And most of the time, it's downright painful to be operating in your zone of incompetence. Think of a painter being asked to audit your books. It's possible, but it's probably not the best use of that person's skills. You do not want to spend much time here, if any.

You will increase the potential for success when you make a commitment not only to show up in your genius, but also to let go of your areas of incompetence, competence, and even excellence. As in every encounter on your journey, your first step is facing, as in getting clear on what you are doing that falls into each of the zones, so you can make a conscious decision on what to let go of and what to step even more fully into. It doesn't serve anybody, especially you, to show up in anything less than your genius.

How My Boss Freed Me Up to Contribute to My Genius

As I mentioned earlier, between the time when I was the director of the Street to Home Initiative in Times Square and the director of the 100,000 Homes Campaign, I served as the director of innovations. As the Street to Home Initiative was nearing its aim of a two-thirds reduction in street homelessness, my boss, Rosanne Haggerty, pulled me aside and said, "You're pretty good at starting up new programs. What if we promoted you to director of innovations and put you in charge of all our new programs?" I eagerly agreed.

Rosanne had no shortage of energy, enthusiasm, new ideas, or new programs.

I'm talking about years of my life when I was waking up in the morning to discover that she had emailed me at 2:00 a.m. with yet another good idea. In many ways, my job was exhilarating. The whole time, Rosanne mentored me and brought me along for all kinds of fantastic work adventures.

But fast-forward a couple years, and I had nine direct reports and was getting burned out. I had bitten off more than I could chew, and I hadn't yet been to the California workshop where I recovered my no. So all I knew to do when she emailed me at 2:00 a.m. with a good idea was to say, "Absolutely, yes. Great idea! We'll do that right away!"

Because I didn't know how to say no yet, I was growing resentful. On many occasions I contemplated quitting my job. I would literally talk to myself on the Q train, rehearsing my inner monologue. "She's going to say this, then I'm going to say that, then she'll say this, then I'll say, 'I quit!'" Talk about being on the Drama Triangle. This is what that looks like, folks!

So one day Rosanne emailed me and said, "Hey, let's talk about how things are going. I'm going to be in SoHo tomorrow afternoon. Can we meet at Dean & DeLuca for coffee around two?"

Going into that meeting, I was absolutely certain that one of two things was going to happen. She was going to fire me, or I was going to quit. Thankfully, Rosanne offered to go first. She started with something along the lines of "Becky, you're one of the best leaders I've ever met."

Me: **sips coffee** *Go on . . .*

She continued: "But you're not a very good manager."

"Yeah, I've thought that myself sometimes."

Then she asked this: "What can we do to free you up from management so that you can really lead? And what would you want to lead if we really freed you up?"

I'll spare you the details of how we reorganized the company, but suffice it to say she didn't fire me, and I didn't quit. But her question changed the course of my life. The 100,000 Homes Campaign ultimately grew out of this meeting. I knew my heart was with street homelessness. I knew I wanted to share what we had learned far beyond Manhattan.

"What can we do to free you up from management so that you can really lead? And what would you want to lead if we really freed you up?"

If you take nothing else from this book, take those two questions and ask them of yourself, and ask them of your colleagues. Notice where your colleagues come to life and free them up to do more of that. It truly might be that simple. There's never any need to blame or criticize. Just free people up to do what they love.

Act Now: What Is Your Genius?

Take a look at your calendar from the past two weeks (assuming they are somewhat typical weeks). Reflect on each thing you did and assign it to one of the zones below. To help determine how you should categorize each of your tasks, ask yourself how you were feeling when you did it. Did you lose track of time? How were the results? Did you experience joy?

GENIUS	EXCELLENCE
COMPETENCE	**INCOMPETENCE**

List your top three genius tasks or ways of being while you were doing those genius tasks:

1. _____
2. _____
3. _____

How can you free yourself up to do more of these three things? Is there anything you can let go of that is not in your genius? Are there any agreements you want to change?

_____
_____

_____

_____

_____

_____

_____

_____

Act Now: Pay It Forward with Your Team Genius Swap

One of the things I do with my teams and encourage all the teams we work with to do is support everyone getting really clear on what genius contributions they'd like to make. Next, we have them get clear on what tasks they are currently doing in their zones of excellence, competence, and incompetence. Then, they do a "genius swap."

My wife, Christine, created this genius swap in which, every couple of months, everyone reflects on where they're at and nominates one thing to come off their plate. So if you're the manager facilitating this, you basically ask your team, "What's the one thing you'd like to come off your plate, and never have to do again?" and have them write that down.

It's your job as the manager to consider whether that activity even really needs to be done. If not, you just take it off the team's list of responsibilities. If it must be done, then offer it up to the team. So, say your team communications director doesn't want to write blog posts anymore. You could ask your team if anyone else is interested. And someone might raise their hand and say, "Oh, I've been meaning to work on my creative writing, and I'd like to give that a try." In that case, even though they're not the communications director, you give them a chance and see what they do with it.

Now, in the case where there are tasks that need to be done but that nobody on the team really wants to do, you do what I call a "genius dump." You take all those tasks and roll them up together, and that becomes the job description for the next hire when you have more money. The new person will be doing all the stuff that nobody else is good at, which actually works really well, because they'll be excited to do it, and everyone else will be excited for them to join and take those tasks off their plates. (I'm sure in some cases there are legal issues or overbearing HR departments, but if you can get away with something like this, go for it!)

If your organization does not yet have the funding to create a new position, but it is clear that doing so will liberate you and your colleagues, my recommendation is to prioritize your fundraising efforts for this new position. It might take a few months, but if this is what wants to happen next, you will be able to find the money.

Genius Clarity and Your Job

Once you've had a little time exploring what your genius is, you'll have a better idea if it really lines up with your job. What if you realize that there's a misalignment between your job and what you really want to express in the world? If the distance between the two is significant, it's possible you may want to try to find a different job. But if there's just a little gap, then you may want to consider making a commitment to yourself to express your genius through your work. This is something where you don't need anybody's permission; you just decide to commit to it and then do it.

All you need is a commitment between you and the universe to express your genius in the world. A great example of this is an acquaintance, Genia Wright, who was the chief operating officer of a really big justice nonprofit. COOs aren't really expected to be funny, but Genia is an improv comedian on the side. She has a lot of genius in operations, but she also brought her genius around humor to the job. She was effective and funny. She didn't limit her genius expression to formal job activities. She layered it in to make a double-genius sandwich. And she didn't need to ask anybody's permission. She just decided that this was what she was going to do.

Another example is Linda, a colleague of mine at the 100,000 Homes Campaign. She realized that even though she had also been a COO for many years, she really didn't like supervising. I thought she was great at supervising and had no idea that for her it was an area of excellence that was burning her out. Feeling responsible for other people was making her tired. One day she came to me in tears and said, "Becky, I need to tell you something. I don't want to supervise anyone anymore." She assumed that meant I would fire her because that's what her job description had consisted of until that point.

I said, "Oh my gosh, what do you *want* to do?" She said she liked traveling and loved getting people excited about our mission, which she also happened to be really good at doing. So I said, "Well, we could use that, too. Why don't you do that full time?" So that became her new job description. We brought in the person she had been supervising, Jessica, and asked her if she was interested in learning how to supervise. She said, "Sure!" and right there in that moment, twenty-five-year-old Jessica became sixty-year-old Linda's team leader. Linda was freed up to contribute from her genius and Jessica got to learn how to be a team leader. And they both lived happily ever after.

So maybe there's a way you can make a commitment to expressing more of your genius through your work. Maybe you need to change some agreements to do so, maybe not. That's for you to discover along the way.

Chapter 11 Takeaways

- Your genius is not only what you do, but how you do it, the essence qualities that you allow to shine through no matter what you are doing.
- Contributing from your genius is a high-leverage way to shift the context by showing up at the intersection of what you're really good at and what you love doing.
- Letting go of struggling in what Gay Hendricks calls your zones of incompetence, competence, and even excellence can have an exponential impact on your success as a social change leader.
- If you want to turbocharge your social change effort, find ways to support your colleagues in showing up more and more in their genius, too.

EPILOGUE

How Do You Take This Forward to Repair the World?

Sometimes, despite all our good looks and personality, despite our best attempts to infuse appreciation, authenticity, healthy agreements, and genius into our work to make the world a better place, we still find ourselves at an impasse. We realize that we cannot do all of this alone.

I've got a secret for you: *nothing really worth doing in terms of social change can be done solo.*

You don't just need your own personal power but also to lock arms in solidarity with others and to activate their personal power, too. That's how large-scale change comes about.

The good news is it is far easier to create an "us" once you've done the inner work and developed the skills we've covered in this book. Everything from facing to embracing to clarifying to shifting will make you a better leader, collaborator, partner, colleague, and friend.

To shift from "me" to "we," take everything you've learned in this book and do it with the important people in your life, especially those who have the potential to be arm in arm with you, endeavoring to repair the world. Let's talk about how to do that.

How to Invite Others to Face What They've Been Avoiding

State your truth, unarguably, and invite others into shared purpose. It cannot be an imposition. It must be an invitation. They must have room to say no. You only want the people who really want to be there. There are more than seven billion people in the world. You will find your people!

Dan and Chip Heath's book *Switch* is an excellent primer for supporting people in making behavior change. They say that first you have to capture people's emotional attention, what they call "motivating the elephant." Ask yourself how you can tap into people's emotions to motivate them to take a risk with you.

Christine Ortiz's "The Problem with Problems" course is also a fantastic resource for getting crystal clear on what problem you're trying to solve in the first place.[7] That's something your team could get started with right away.

LaShawn Chatmon and Kathleen Osta with the National Equity Project taught me that when we're doing real social justice work, it's absolutely essential that we slow down and make time for relationships. When you're bringing people together, do not jam-pack your agenda. Create time and space for the deep and important work of being with one another in addition to the important work of doing things together. One of the most powerful ways I've learned to support emotional authenticity and the development of bonds between people is to do Marshall Ganz and the New Organizing Institute's Public Narrative work together. When our Billions Institute Fellows met for the very first retreat, literally all we did was share our stories with one another. For three days. That's it. Nothing else on the agenda. When it was over, some people started crying,

---

7. You can take Christine Ortiz's course here: https://courses
.equitymeetsdesign.com/p/the-problem-with-problems.

saying they didn't want to leave. This is the power of authentic stories and slowing down.

How to Help Members of Your Team Embrace Their Power

Unwinding the tentacles of oppression and marginalization that seep into even the most conscientious organizations is the specific expertise of some of our faculty and fellows and many other organizations that have much more to contribute about this than I ever could. Many of the people I've mentioned throughout this book do this, and they are really good at it. These people include Susan Jane with Navigators Consulting; my wife, Christine Margiotta, with Social Justice Partners; Lindsay Hill with Sojourner Advising; Michelle Molitor with The Equity Lab; Christine Ortiz with Equity Meets Design; Heather Kawamoto with Collective Liberation LLC; and LaShawn Chatmon and Kathleen Osta with the National Equity Project.

I highly encourage you to bring in experts like these and give this the attention it deserves. Meanwhile, humility, curiosity, and courage can help you get started.

How to Help Your Team Clarify Their Commitment

What is each member's individual commitment, and what are your shared aims and purpose? This is one of the few areas where taking the time to build consensus will really pay off in the long run. Slow down, take the time to really listen to one another, and discover shared purpose, while allowing plenty of space for each person to come to the work from their own unique commitment.

Frances Olajide taught us that at the end of each Billions Institute large-scale change workshop, we should write one word on a smooth stone to capture and remind ourselves of what we're committing to take forward into the world. This can be a powerful ritual for capturing the commitment of each member of your team. Or you could all go out and get tattoos together. Maybe do the rock thing.

How Can You Shift the Overall Context and Do the Work of Repairing the World?

Donella Meadows writes about changing paradigms in her seminal article, "Leverage Points: Places to Intervene in a System." There's nothing necessarily physical or expensive or even slow in the process of paradigm change. In a single individual it can happen in a millisecond. All it takes is a click in the mind, a falling of scales from eyes, a new way of seeing. So, too, can you shift the context:

One choice at a time.

One commitment at a time.

One unarguable reveal at a time.

One request at a time.

One agreement at a time.

Appreciation all the time.

Genius all the time.

Lather. Rinse. Repeat.

Big social change is nothing more, really, than a bunch of people coming together to face something that no longer works for them and then working to change a collective agreement. That's it, really. There are some other strategies and tactics that will help organize your work, and we teach those, too. But really, in its essence, social change is about facing and changing implicit societal agreements, together, in solidarity.

It is one of the most wildly creative and joyful things you could possibly do with your life. And it will challenge you to your core. My greatest hope is that this book will guide you in being able to reliably bring your whole and best self to making whatever dent in the universe you are determined to make. I hope this book is dog-eared and has a tattered cover by the time you lend it to another change leader and insist that they give it back when they're done reading it. Or even better, that they pass it along to another change leader who could use a boost.

Never, ever doubt that you are more than enough. You, deeply grounded in your essence, fully aligned with your commitment, courageously creating new contexts—you in your wholeness—are ultimately what repairs the world. May we all thrive in answering the call.

Onward!

ACKNOWLEDGMENTS

My friend Susan X Jane once remarked that our areas of incompetence are where we need community. As I reflect on the magnitude of contributions from so many people, I am well aware that writing a book is not quite in my zone of genius. I am humbled and overwhelmed with gratitude for the community that came together to create this book. I see this book as a packaged gift from all of us to each of you.

Over a series of months, I typed up what Anne Lamott calls a "shitty first draft" and Kate Rouze followed behind me, magically retaining my voice but with a lot more pith. And although it happened quite organically, it turns out this book in its structure and approach is an adaptation of the Hendricks Institute's F.A.C.T. process (where "F.A.C.T." stands for "Facing, Accepting, Choosing, and Taking Action.") You can find that entire F.A.C.T. process in its original format in appendix A. In fact, you will find many references to Kathlyn Hendricks throughout this book. In many ways, I see this book as a distillation of what I learned during an apprenticeship with her, adapted and translated to be relevant to the people I know and love most: those of us committed to making the world a better place. I cannot overstate how grateful I am for Kathlyn's mentorship and friendship, not to mention her generosity in providing feedback over multiple drafts of this book and writing the foreword. She and her husband, Gay, have been exploring the concept of responsibility and shifting contexts for over four decades now. Without her, this would not have been possible.

Once we had a solid first draft complete, I asked some friends and colleagues for feedback: Selena Liu Raphael, Mike Thompson, Susan Rivers, Leslie Chertok, Nicole Taylor, Neela Rajendra, Eunice Lin Nichols, Joe McCannon, Daisy Sharrock, Parvathi Santhosh-Kumar, Kate Hilton, Michelle Pledger, Mari Jones, Dan Heath, Erika Cravalho-Meyers, Tatiana Fox, and Neil Gordon. This is a much more useful book because of their input.

I am aware that my privileged identity increases the likelihood that someday there will be a review along the lines of "This is all well and good if you're a well-off white lady." I'm also aware of the possibility that I may have unknowingly appropriated wisdom or practices that are sacred to another culture without acknowledging them as such. My fifty-plus years of socialization as a white person in the United States make it likely that I will miss or misunderstand some important truths, be completely unaware in my communications, or not understand what someone else is experiencing.

Knowing that the way I think about things is shaped by my privileged identity, and therefore limited and incomplete, I hired five people who have expertise in advancing racial and social justice to offer critique and feedback: Michelle Molitor, Katie Hong, Lindsay Hill, Heather Kawamoto, and Susan X Jane. I want this book to be as relevant and useful as possible, and I know we cannot make lasting change without also addressing systems of oppression, which is not my area of expertise. I humbly asked for their advice. I asked them to rip the first draft of this book to shreds. And thank goodness they did!

Interestingly, the experts didn't always agree with one another. When I received conflicting advice, I picked up the phone, asked for further clarification, and then made the best call I could at the time. I am especially grateful for the depth and breadth of Susan X Jane's feedback, which profoundly deepened the narrative in this book.

Since each of the race and equity experts I brought into this project had different perspectives and experiences, I am pretty sure you will, too. And though I hope with their help we were able to make this book useful beyond my demographic doppelgangers, I know that I still have so much to learn. So please don't hesitate to send me a note at becky@billionsinstitute .com, because I'm still learning, and I will receive your feedback as the gift that it is.

This book would not be possible without the genius contributions of the team at Girl Friday Productions, including Leslie Ann Miller, who believed in it enough to take it on as a project; Jennifer Dorsey and Michael Schuler, whose editing took this to a new level; Sara Spees Addicott, who kept the trains running on time; and Georgie Hockett and her brilliant marketing team, who brought some pizzazz to the party.

My final reader was my wife and partner, Christine Margiotta, who encouraged me to write this book in the first place, read it multiple times, and gave me feedback with a fine-tuned equity lens, too. Christine is my number-one confidante and advisor. Her thumbprints are all over this book and her influence is woven throughout. It is to Christine, and the two amazing human beings she brought into this world, our children, Huck and Vivian, that I dedicate this book.

February 15, 2021

Written on the traditional, ancestral, and unceded Indigenous land of the Gabrielino/Tongva peoples, in what is called by some Claremont, California.

APPENDIX A

F.A.C.T. Process from the Hendricks Institute

Practicing Presence with F.A.C.T.
Facing | Accepting | Choosing | Taking Action

Facilitator: practice your loop with curiosity and appreciation throughout the process.

F *Turn toward your issue/item, then turn away. Explore the different ways you do and could face and avoid facing for a minute or two.*

Then choose to turn fully toward and open your body.

Create a pleasant hmmm through an out breath and then ask, "What about this haven't I fully faced directly?" and notice your whole-body response.

A *Relax your breath by tightening your belly muscles slightly on the out breath and opening your belly like a balloon filling on the in breath.*

When you feel your breath slowing and opening, ask yourself: "What's the hardest thing to accept about all this?"

Let one hand hold and express with movement while you say, "Yes, I want to accept," and let the other hold and express while you say, "and I don't want to accept this."

To continue, you could say "I'm willing to accept and I'm scared."

Have the client express with both hands several times until an experience of flow or shifting happens.

C *Sound the pleasurable hmmm again with your out breaths as you create small, new, and friendly movements with your fingers, hands, and arms, while asking yourself... "What do I really want about all this?"*

Ask out loud several times emphasizing different words and using different tones of voice until you feel a whole-body shift toward openness.

T *Let yourself hmmm easily while moving around the room and asking yourself, "What's the simplest, most pleasurable action step you can take that will lead you toward what you really want?"*

What? And by when?

APPENDIX B

Persona Interview from the Hendricks Institute

The Persona Interview, created by Gay and Kathlyn Hendricks, is one of my favorite tools for efficiently and effectively shifting from a persona back into my essence. The beauty of this activity is that all you have to do is do it. There's nothing to fix. Nothing else to do other than bring your loving, curious attention to whatever persona is making an appearance right now.

So pick a persona you'd like to shift, give that persona a name, find a friend, and ask them to ask you these questions, using the persona name where the blanks are. Your job is to simply blurt out the first answer that comes to your consciousness. Don't hold it too tightly—just blurt it out and let it go. The results are from doing the process itself, not the actual answers per se.

_____, what is the most important thing to you?

_____, what are you most proud of?

_____, when did you make your first appearance?

_____, who did you learn your style from?

_____, what are you most afraid of?

_____, what do you most want?

© 2003 Hendricks Institute

Once the interview is complete, shake it off, and appreciate yourself for being willing to shift. Then go on with your life!

If you'd like to see an example of how to do a Persona Interview, you can check out a demonstration online at www .billionsinstitute.com/persona-interview.

ABOUT THE AUTHOR

Photo © Lara Jenkins

Becky Margiotta is the cofounder of the Billions Institute and host of the podcast *Unleashing Social Change*. She has trained thousands of people the world over on how to design and lead large-scale social change.

Margiotta directed the 100,000 Homes Campaign for Community Solutions, which mobilized 186 cities to permanently house more than one hundred thousand people who had previously been living on their streets. Her work has been profiled on *60 Minutes*, NPR, the *New York Times*, the *Washington Post*, the *Stanford Social Innovation Review*, and the *Harvard Business Review*. A graduate of West Point, she also served for nine years as an officer in the US Army, both in Special Operations and Special Mission Units. She earned a master's degree in organizational change management from The New School University and has received a White House Champion of Change award, the Schwab Foundation's Social Entrepreneur of the Year award, and the National Conference on Citizenship's HOOAH Award. She lives in Claremont, California, with her wife and their two kids.